EDWARD S. CURTIS IN THE LAND OF THE WAR CANOES

Thomas Burke Memorial Washington State Museum   MONOGRAPH 2

Thomas Burke Memorial Washington State Museum Monographs

1. Northwest Coast Indian Art: An Analysis of Form, *by Bill Holm*
2. Edward S. Curtis in the Land of the War Canoes: A Pioneer Cinematographer in the Pacific Northwest, *by Bill Holm and George Irving, Quimby*

Edward S. Curtis in the Land of the War Canoes

A PIONEER CINEMATOGRAPHER IN THE PACIFIC NORTHWEST

Bill Holm and George Irving Quimby

UNIVERSITY OF WASHINGTON PRESS   *Seattle and London*

Copyright © 1980 by the University of Washington Press
Printed in the United States of America
Designed by Audrey Meyer

Library of Congress Cataloging in Publication Data

Holm, Bill, 1925–
    Edward S. Curtis in the land of the war canoes.

    (Thomas Burke Memorial Washington State Museum
monograph ; 2)
    1. Curtis, Edward S., 1868–1952. 2. Cinematogra-
phers—United States—Biography. I. Quimby, George
Irving, 1913–   joint author. II. Title.
III. Series: Washington (State). University.
Museum. Monograph ; 2.
TR849.C87H64   1980   778.5'3'0924   80–12172
ISBN 0–295–95708–5

The title page ornament represents Thunderbird's
breastplate (see houseposts, p. 54). *Drawing by
Bill Holm*

Preface

In 1914 Edward S. Curtis made the first full-length documentary motion picture of aboriginal North Americans. Although he was a pioneer cinematographer, little is known of that aspect of his professional life. Between 1967 and 1974 we restored the Curtis motion picture, edited the original footage, added a sound track, and changed the title from *In the Land of the Head-Hunters* to *In the Land of the War Canoes* (see chap. 6). In restoring his movie we began to learn about Curtis, the man, and decided that we wanted to learn more. We also felt an obligation to historians of cinematography to record what we did to the original Curtis film as well as why and how we did it. Accordingly, we began our additional research and the writing of this book in the summer of 1974, and continued with new and important bits and pieces of information through the summer of 1979.

It is not our purpose here to attempt to place Edward Curtis in the history of cinematography; our aim is to provide the data by means of which qualified historians might place him in that history. Also it is not our intent to evaluate Curtis in the hierarchy of anthropologists of his day. Suffice it to say that we consider him a good ethnographer, and admire the quality of his work among the Kwakiutl.

In the course of our research and writing we believe that we got to know Edward Curtis very well, even to the point that we imagined ourselves to be a part of the Curtis team whose members always called him Chief. And in this imagined position we believe that we were able to separate fact from fiction.

In his later years, without the constraints of scientific ethnography and the rigorous editing of William E. Myers and F. W. Hodge, Curtis, perhaps with artistic license, embellished some of his tales beyond the limits of historical accuracy. Among his favorite stories were the night on Devil Rock, the encounter with an octopus, and the smashing of his canoe by a whale. They are, however, great stories. In fact, he had enough real adventures and close calls in his brilliant and exciting career that he had no need of the apocryphal embellishments, except perhaps as exercises in the writing of adventure stories or as public relations efforts on behalf of the Curtis Studio. In any event, we agree with his daughter Florence that Edward Curtis was a genius and can only add, Chief, it has for us been a pleasure and an adventure to edit your old motion picture film and to write a book about you.

Acknowledgments

Among the many Kwakiutl people from whom over a number of years Bill Holm gathered information on traditional native life, the following furnished important material related directly to Curtis, his work among the Kwakiutl, and the interpretation of his Kwakiutl photographs and motion picture film: George Cadwallader,* Agnes Cranmer, Katherine Ferry, Margaret Frank, Charlie George, Dorothy Hawkins,* Jonathan Hunt,* Thomas Hunt, Emma Hunt, Mary Johnson,* Helen Knox, Herbert Martin,* Mungo Martin,* William Scow, Joe Seaweed, Willie Seaweed,* James Sewid, Peter S. Smith,* Dick Willie,* Tom Willie, and Bob Wilson.*

A number of other persons were very helpful to us. Mick Gidley, Senior Lecturer in American Literature at the University of Exeter, England and Visiting Scholar at the Burke Museum, University of Washington, during the academic year of 1976–77, provided us with a wide range of useful information and helped with the organization of our material. Curtis' daughter, Florence Curtis Graybill of Laguna Hills, California, gave us important details about her father. Teri C. McLuhan of New York City supplied us with data and leads to information about Curtis as a cinematographer. Peter Macnair, Curator of Ethnology at the Provincial Museum, Victoria, British Columbia, arranged for the use of museum facilities in time of need. Don Lelooska gave us permission to use the George Hunt account book, which is in his possession. Gerald H. Grosso, Conservator at the Neah Bay Laboratory of the Ozette Archaeological Project, kindly provided us with information concerning the Curtis homestead at Port Orchard, which he copied from old legal records. Robert D. Monroe, Head of the Special Collections Division of the University of Washington Library, supplied us with old newspaper accounts of Curtis and his adventures and accomplishments. Andrew F. Johnson, Librarian, and Susan E. Cunningham, Library Technician, Northwest Collections, University of Washington Library, supplied us with working space and books, most of which were very heavy. We thank them all.

* deceased

Contents

A Note on the Photographs

During the production of Edward Curtis' documentary moving picture on the Kwakiutl Indians, one of Curtis' chief assistants, Edmund August Schwinke, made his own private record of the filming. With a 1903 Eastman Kodak camera, Schwinke shot Edward Curtis behind his movie camera; George Hunt, megaphone in hand, directing the actors; and the actors themselves, relaxing between takes. These photographs only came to light in 1977 and were obtained by the Burke Museum, University of Washington. They have shed a great deal of light on Curtis' techniques of filmmaking, and because Schwinke identified his photographs by month and year of exposure (chiefly May, June, and July of 1914), we have important information on the chronology of the filming.

Most of the illustrations in this volume are Edmund Schwinke's photographs, published here for the first time. Combined with a number of prints made from frames in the film itself and Edward S. Curtis photographs of the Kwakiutl, these illustrations offer an exciting view of an early ethnographic film venture. Given their historical importance, we have included a few even though they have lost some of their sharpness of detail because the surviving print was faded or scratched.

As a guide to the source of the illustrations, the following key has been used in the captions:

[Curtis]   Photographs by Edward S. Curtis from volume 10 of *The North American Indian* (figs. 6, 9, 14, 34, 39, 41, 53, 55)

[Head-Hunters]   Illustrations from the 1914 publication *In the Land of the Head-Hunters* by Edward S. Curtis (Yonkers-on-Hudson, N.Y.: World Book Company) (figs. 3, 10, 15, 29, 33, 50)

[Holm]   Photograph by Bill Holm (fig. 2)

[LC]   Prints from film footage of *In the Land of the Head-Hunters* in the Library of Congress (figs. 27, 30, 31, 32, 38, 42, 49, 54, 57)

[MPM]   Photographs courtesy of the Milwaukee Public Museum, Milwaukee, Wisconsin (figs. 7, 11)

[Putnam]   Photograph by John Putnam (fig. 8)

[Schwinke]   Photographs by Edmund August Schwinke (figs. 5, 12, 13, 16, 17, 18, 19, 20, 21, 22, 23, 24, 25, 26, 28, 35, 36, 37, 40, 43, 44, 45, 46, 47, 48, 51, 52, 56)

[UW Photo Coll.]   Document courtesy Photography Collection, University of Washington Library (fig. 1)

Illustrations

EDWARD S. CURTIS IN THE LAND OF THE WAR CANOES

Edward Sheriff Curtis, self-portrait, 1899

I. Introduction

This book is about Edward Sheriff Curtis, a man of genius: pioneer photographer, author, and motion picture maker. He lived in the Pacific Northwest from 1887 to 1920, and during this period became internationally famous for his artistic and scholarly works, chiefly a twenty-volume work on aboriginal Indian life in North America and a full-length motion picture of the Kwakiutl.

Curtis' *The North American Indian* consisted of twenty volumes of text printed on imported hand-made paper of the best quality. Each volume, bound in irregularly grained morocco leather, contained about three hundred pages of text and photogravure prints. There were fifteen hundred prints in the twenty volumes. Moreover, each volume was accompanied by a corresponding portfolio containing thirty-six or more copperplate photogravures, measuring 12 × 16 inches, on 18 × 22 inch sheets printed on special paper. There were 722 of these plates in the twenty portfolios.

This magnificent example of the bookmaker's art was costly to produce, and costly to purchase. Each set of twenty volumes and accompanying portfolios was priced at three thousand to forty-five hundred dollars. The volumes and portfolios were published from 1907 to 1930 and at least two hundred sets were sold through subscription to museums and wealthy patrons. The first volume includes an appreciation of Edward Curtis written by the President of the United States, Theodore Roosevelt. He wrote in part as follows:

In Mr. Curtis we have both an artist and a trained observer, . . . [who] because of the singular combination of qualities with which he has been blest, and because of his extraordinary success in making and using his opportunities, has been able to do what no other man could do. . . . He has lived on intimate terms with many different tribes of the mountains and the plains. He knows them as they hunt, as they travel, as they go about their various avocations on the march and in the camp. He knows their medicine men and their sorcerers, their chiefs and warriors, their young men and maidens. He has not only seen their vigorous outward existence, but has caught glimpses, such as few white men ever catch, into that strange spiritual and mental life of theirs; from whose innermost recesses all white men are forever barred. Mr. Curtis . . . is rendering a real and great service . . . not only to our own people, but to the world of scholarship everywhere.

Clearly Curtis' greatest accomplishment was *The North American Indian*. His next greatest achievement was a full-length motion picture—the first of its kind—about the aboriginal life of the Kwakiutl, a spectacular maritime people of the Northwest Coast, vastly different from the tribes of the mountains and the plains.

The film had a short burst of glory and then, for unknown reasons, faded from sight for many years. It was shown publicly shortly after it was finished in 1914, first at the Casino in New York and later at the Moore Theater in Seattle. A glowing review of the New York screening by the motion picture critic W. Stephen Bush appeared in *The Moving Picture World*, and poet Vachel Lindsay mentioned the film with favor in his book *The Art of the Moving Picture* (1915). Lindsay wrote: "The photoplay of the American Indian should in most instances be planned as bronze in action. . . . Mr. Edward S. Curtis, the super-photographer, has made an Ethnological collection of photographs of our American Indians. This work of a lifetime, a supreme art achievement, shows the native as a figure in bronze. Mr. Curtis' photoplay, *The Land of the Head Hunters . . .* , a romance of the Indians of the North-West, abounds in whole bronzes" (1922:86).

W. Stephen Bush's 1914 review of the film provides an even greater sense of the artistic importance of Curtis in his day:

I remember many efforts to make the life of remote countries and strange tribes live on the screen. I remember how the attempt was made to get the natives into a moving picture scenario and thus render the film more acceptable. It is not a pleasing recollection by any means because all these efforts were strikingly futile. Mr. Curtis has found the short cut of genius and he eminently succeeds where others have dismally failed. It is said that Mr. Curtis is a profound student of Indian lore. This is evident enough from the films, but it does not at all explain his success with this subject on the screen. The cause of that must be sought in an extraordinary perception of artistic and dramatic values, in an uncommon skill of selection and in a sort of second sight with the camera. . . . [The film] has brought before my eyes a new vista of camera miracles. . . .
Mr. Curtis conceived this wonderful study in ethnology as an epic. It fully deserves the name. Indeed, it seemed to me that there was a most striking resemblance all through the film between the musical epics of Richard Wagner and the theme and treatment of this Indian epic. The fire dance, the vigil journey with its command of silence and chastity, the whole character of the hero were most strangely reminiscent of Parsifal and the Ring of the Nibelungs. . . .
I speak advisedly when I say that this production sets a new mark in artistic handling of films in which educational values mingle with dramatic interest. Even the scene showing the head-hunters is redeemed from the gruesome by the exceeding skill which characterizes the production as a whole. "In the Land of the Head Hunters" is a title which does not begin to describe all the film contains. It is not a feature for the nickelodeon or the cheap house, but it ought to be welcomed by the better class of houses that are looking for an occasional departure from the regular attractions and that want to give their patrons a special treat [1914:1685].

One would be hard pressed to find a more glowing review, with such a string of superlatives. Bush calls the film "a gem of the motion picture art . . . [that] has never been surpassed." He even gives Curtis full credit for the quality of acting of the Indian participants when he writes, "The Indian mind is, I believe, constitutionally incapable of acting; it cannot even grasp the meaning of acting as we understand it. Probably nobody understands this fact better than Mr. Curtis." How little Bush knew of Kwakiutl culture! Their ceremonial life is a series of dramatic festivals, the most important of which—the Winter Ceremony—is called by the Kwakiutl "Tseyka." The word is difficult to translate, but most informants agree that it refers to the dramatization of the power and actions of the spirits which motivate the festival, and it can be translated simply "acting."

Despite the accolades, *In the Land of the Head-Hunters* was for all practical purposes lost to the world from shortly after it was made in 1914 until the late 1940s when a print came into the possession of the Field Museum in Chicago.[1] At that time George Quimby was curator of exhibits in the Museum's Department of Anthropology. Familiar with Curtis' *North American Indian*, he immediately recognized the similarities between the images of the film and the illustrations in the tenth volume of Curtis' work.

The print was 35mm nitrate film in very poor shape, with sections faded, scratched, crazed, and brittle. Various parts of the film were tinted in colors—red, green, and sepia—to fit the mood of particular scenes. The original title and credits were missing, but one subtitle in boldface, "The Vigil of Motana," was mistakenly thought to be the title of the whole film until 1966 when the Moore Theater handbill, giving the full title, was found (fig. 1).

In 1948 the film was shown for a small group of personnel in the Field Museum's theater. Fortunately the projection booth was properly equipped for the screening of the highly flammable film of early motion picture days because the film caught fire and the operator had to make a fireman's escape down the ladder-like stairway to avoid the poisonous fumes of the burning nitrate. An automatic damper on the projector snuffed out the fire and little footage was lost, but the warning was

1. In the autumn of 1947 a collector of old movies, Hugo Zeiter of Danville, Illinois, donated a print of *In the Land of the Head-Hunters* to the Field Museum.

clear. The film was transferred to 16mm safety film, and the old nitrate film was destroyed.

Another twenty-five years elapsed before the film was again ready to show to the audiences which Curtis had hoped to reach in 1914. In this interval virtually none of the admirers of his work were aware that he had made a motion picture.

About 1948 George Quimby had asked Kenneth Macgowan, chairman of theater arts at the University of California at Los Angeles, an authority on motion pictures and himself a producer, to make a search of records for any listing of Curtis' work. The search turned up nothing. As late as 1972, A. D. Coleman wrote, "It is to be regretted that Curtis finished his work before making movies. . . . his flair for the dramatic would have made him a marvelous filmmaker, and the Indians surely needed a spokesman in the early days of the film. Many of his images, in fact, seem like stills from a film" (Coleman and McLuhan 1972:vii).

Curtis had expected *In the Land of the Head-Hunters* to be a great financial success. Why did the film fail to live up to his optimistic prophecy? Why did Robert Flaherty's *Nanook of the North*, made eight years later and conceptually much like Curtis' film in its reconstruction of an earlier phase of a tribal culture, become a timeless classic while *In the Land of the Head-Hunters* was forgotten? At the time we restored and edited his film in 1973, the name of Edward Curtis did not appear in any published history of the motion picture. The reasons for this almost total lack of recognition will probably never be known.

Since the discovery of the existence of the film, Quimby had been interested in trying to restore it.[2] The 16mm version at silent speed

2. At the time Quimby was working on plans for reinstalling exhibits in three large halls in the Field Museum devoted to the North American Indians. One of these halls was to contain exhibits of Northwest Coast Indian culture and Quimby proposed to use the Curtis film as part of the exhibition, incorporating appropriate segments of the film into individual exhibits dealing with canoes and their use, dances, and masks and costumes. This hall was never completed, but a similar plan has been considered for the Thomas Burke Memorial Washington State Museum.

MOORE THEATER

December 7 to 15—Matinees Daily

The World Film Corporation

presents

In the Land of the Head Hunters

A Drama of Primitive Life on the Shores of the North Pacific
From Story Written and Picture Made by
EDWARD S. CURTIS

Every Participant an Indian and Every Incident True to Native Life.
Produced by the Seattle Film Co., Inc.
Interpretive Music Composed by John J. Braham from Phonographic Records of Indian Music.
Printing and Color Effects by Pierson Laboratories, Hochsteter Process.
Border Designs by Dugald Walker.
Cyclorama Stage Sets by Co-Operative Producing Company, executed by Frank Cambria.

1. *Moore Theater (Seattle) handbill of 1914. [UW Photo Coll.]*

was jerky, with abrupt shifts from light to dark. He wisely did not tackle this project in the late 1940s or early 1950s, however, because the technology for extensive restoration did not exist. In 1965 when he left the Field Museum to come two thousand miles closer to the Northwest Coast, he brought with him carefully made copies of the footage, which the Museum had given him permission to restore. At the University of Washington, where he became curator of ethnology at the Thomas Burke Memorial Washington State Museum, he had an opportunity to collaborate with Bill Holm, an expert on Kwakiutl culture, also greatly interested in the film.

In 1956 Bill Holm had begun a long and rewarding association with the Kwakiutl people of northern Vancouver Island, the same people who had so intrigued Curtis years before. Over the years of this association, Holm had been impressed by recurring references to Curtis, and especially to the film he had made at Fort Rupert. Old people who remembered Curtis and his filming were full of anecdotes about the work. None had ever seen the film and all were curious about it. Holm's own curiosity grew and he began his search for a print, asking filmmakers, librarians, museum curators, or anyone else who might know of the existence of the film. The older Kwakiutl were dying one by one and he hoped to find a copy to show to them before the last of Curtis' generation was gone.

In August of 1962, at the very beginning of a leave Holm had taken for research on Kwakiutl ceremonialism, Chief Mungo Martin died. Mungo Martin had often spoken about Curtis, and Holm had hoped to be able to get his opinion of the film, if it ever turned up. Now that chance was gone. In the course of his research that September, Holm visited the Field Museum in Chicago where he met George Quimby and told him of his search for the mysterious Curtis film and his desire to show it to the Kwakiutl people. Holm told Quimby that he had just come from the funeral of one of the best potential informants on the subject and he was afraid time was very short. When, to his great surprise, Quimby produced the film, they knew their mutual dream

of restoring the film and bringing it back into public view was finally realizable.

In the summer of 1967 Bill Holm, his wife Marty, and his daughters, Carla, seven, and Karen, five, sailed north in their sloop with a 16mm projector, a big reel of film, and the great anticipation of finally moving on the long-awaited project. They visited the places where the film had been shot fifty-three years before and even searched out some of the very rocks where the hero and his father had posed for Curtis' camera (figs. 2 and 3). In all, they showed the film fifteen times in the villages of Alert Bay, Port Hardy, Fort Rupert, Turnour Island, New Vancouver, and Kingcome Inlet, as well as in Victoria. Of the many people who saw the film, some as often as five or six times, over fifty were qualified to comment on the film and many did. A number of them had participated in making the original picture and others had been present at the filming. But there were also some who had died in the preceding years who might have been able to give valuable information.

Many people recalled amusing incidents during the filming: how a dancer in a canoe fell when the canoe struck a rock, how Curtis paid the men to shave off their mustaches, and how the unfamiliar old style abalone-shell nose rings tickled! Holm was encouraged to believe, by the ad-libbing of the audience and the singing which began spontaneously during some of the scenes, that a sound track could be made for the film. He asked several people what they thought of the idea and all were enthusiastic.

In the spring of 1972 financial backing for work on the Curtis film made it possible to record the necessary sound under the direction of David Gerth, a young filmmaker from the Rice University Media Center in Houston, Texas. Holm had arranged with a group of Kwakiutl to record the dialogue and songs in Port Hardy, at the north end of Vancouver Island, in the summer of 1972. Only days before the time set for the recording session a prominent man was accidently killed, and most of the Kwakiutl who were involved in the recording traveled to Comox for the funeral. While that funeral was in progress another prominent person, a much beloved woman, died in Victoria, so the mourners left one funeral for another. The sound technicians were "somewhere" on Vancouver Island—incommunicado—headed for Port Hardy. Holm finally managed to locate David Gerth and his crew, and reluctantly told them to turn around and come back the three hundred miles to Victoria. They arrived the next morning and the recording was completed that day in the Newcombe Auditorium of the British Columbia Provincial Museum. Three of the old people in the recording session were actors in the original film. Present for the recording session were Henry Bell, Dusty Cadwallader, Agnes Cranmer, Jonathan Hunt, Tom Hunt, Emma Hunt, James King, Helen Knox, Katie Scow, Peter Smith, and Bob Wilson. All had previously seen the film, but it was shown again so that everyone could fix the story in mind and catch the mood. Then the first scene was projected several times, until those viewing had had a chance to think through and discuss the appropriate dialogue or song. Finally the scene was projected and the actors spoke their lines. The recording was spontaneous; there was no script or any rigid plan. Elizabeth Waite filled in some gaps in the dialogue in a later recording session.

Since the shots in the film are relatively short, the actors were never finished speaking or singing at the end of a scene, and kept right on until the logical conclusion of the activity. This gave David Gerth and his sound technicians a great deal of tape footage for each scene and allowed a certain amount of selection of appropriate material to fit the visual action. The results exceeded expectations.

The sound crew then went over to Lopez Island where Holm had a thirty-five-foot canoe similar to those used in the film. The canoe was launched with the sound crew aboard and, under the command of Steve Brown, put through all its paces: fast paddling, slow paddling, rounding a point, landing on gravel beaches, shoving off, turning around. Hundreds of feet of tape were recorded, and from that footage, Gerth selected the sounds to be synchronized with the film. The viewer would be hard put to believe those paddle strokes were not recorded in 1914. Gerth also recorded the sounds of surf and waves, wind, fire, birds, and every other sound needed for the final mixing and synchronizing.

In the meantime, the 16mm film taken from the 35mm nitrate film was optically stretched by double-printing every other frame so that it could be projected at sound speed of twenty-four frames per second, rather than at the silent speed of sixteen frames per second. Frames that were too dark were made lighter and those too light were somehow darkened. Parts of sequences that were out of place were put in proper order and David Gerth cleverly extended some sequences that were obviously abrupt because of missing footage by adding frames from a duplicate negative. This system worked especially well in scenes where a figure was standing still or a canoe was viewed in the distance. The film's defects were corrected as much as possible, producing a film that, technically, was a vast improvement over the original Field Museum footage.

Finally, Gerth synchronized each of five different sound tracks with the film, and mixed the five into a single track which was combined with the film. The result seemed miraculous. The combination of image and sound maintained the artistic integrity of Edward Curtis the photographer, and the magnificent cultural heritage of the Kwakiutl Indians. The restored film enhanced by sound has an operatic quality reminiscent of W. Stephen Bush's vision of the movie when he reviewed it in New York City in 1914.

2. *In 1967, while visiting the Kwakiutl villages with the unedited Curtis film, Marty Holm and her daughter Carla struck the poses of Kenada and Motana on the rocks at Deer Island in 1914 (cf. facing fig.). [Holm]*

3. *The hero Motana (Stanley Hunt) and his father Kenada (Paddy Maleed) seated on the rocks on the shore of Deer Island. The largest house pole in the imitation village can be seen in the background,* left. *[Head-Hunters]*

II. Beginnings: 1868–1909

Edward Sheriff Curtis was born in Wisconsin on 19 February 1868. One biographer states he was born on a farm near Whitewater in Walworth County (Andrews 1962:17), but Curtis himself claimed to have been born in Madison, the capital city.[1] By the time Edward was of school age the Curtis family had moved from Wisconsin to the village of Cordova in LeSueur County, Minnesota. There Curtis grew to young manhood. He became a self-taught photographer by studying *Wilson's Photographics: A Series of Lessons Accompanied by Notes on All the Processes Which Are Needful in the Art of Photography*, first printed in 1881. Curtis constructed his own camera using the lens of his father's stereopticon and two wooden boxes, one inside the other. He learned to take pictures and develop negatives and print films. On the basis of this early experience he was able to get a job with a photographic company in St. Paul, Minnesota, where, for more than a year, he worked in the darkroom printing and coating photographic paper and taking a few photographs.

Curtis' father, Johnson Asahel Curtis, a veteran of the Civil War and a minister of the United Brethren Church, was in poor health and far from wealthy. He aimed to improve his health and financial position by moving to Washington Territory. Accordingly, Johnson Curtis, accompanied by his son Edward, left Cordova in 1887 and settled on a homestead in Sidney (now called Port Orchard) where he hoped to establish a brickyard. Edward was nineteen years old at that time. In the spring of 1888, Mrs. Ellen Sheriff Curtis, Ray, twenty-six years old, Eva, seventeen, and Asahel, thirteen, joined Johnson and Edward at Sidney.

The Curtis family lived in a log house built by Edward and his father. There was a large fireplace later fondly recalled by Eva Curtis in her interviews with Ralph W. Andrews (1962:18). Vegetables and fruit trees on the homestead supplied some of the food for the family, and the Curtis boys fished and dug clams, cut firewood for home and sale, and undertook odd jobs for hire. In brief, it was a pioneer existence softened by the abundance of the Puget Sound area and the mild climate. But the bright prospects envisioned by Johnson Curtis never materialized for him. Within a few years he died of pneumonia and the brickyard he was acquiring never became the success of which he long had dreamed. During this period in Sidney, Edward was taking pictures but had not yet become the full-time photographer that he wished to be.

In 1891 Edward Curtis moved to Seattle and became a partner of Rasmus Rothi in the firm of Rothi and Curtis, Photographers. With money obtained by mortgaging part of the Sidney homestead, Curtis had purchased an interest in the firm from Peter H. Sanstrom, an old friend from Cordova, Minnesota, who had also moved to Washington Territory. Curtis parted company with Rasmus Rothi in 1893, however, and entered into a new partnership with Thomas H. Guptil. The new firm on Second Avenue was listed as "Curtis and Guptill, Photographers and Photo-engravers." The 1894–95 *Seattle City Directory* ran a small

---

1. By 1913 Edward Curtis was famous enough to be included in *Who's Who in America*. Since those included ordinarily supplied the information for their listing, the sketch represents what Curtis had to say about himself at that time. He listed himself as an author and said he was born in Madison, Wisconsin. Curtis was a member of the Archaeological Institute of America and the National Geographic Society, the American Alpine Club, the Vagabonds, Mazama, Rainier Club, Arctic Club, and the National Arts Club of New York City. He listed himself as a Republican.

advertisement on its front cover and a more elaborate one inside (in color), extolling Curtis and Guptil as producing the "finest photographic work in the city" (fig. 4).

Edward Curtis had married Clara J. Phillips in June of 1892, and in 1894 they bought a home where they were joined by others of the Curtis family: Asahel, an engraver for Curtis and Guptil; Eva, a teacher; and the widow, Ellen Curtis. Only two years later Curtis had moved again as his household expanded. In residence now was Edward, his wife and children, his brother, sister, and mother, as well as some of his wife's relations, including his sister-in-law, Susie Phillips, a photo-printer at Curtis and Guptil; another sister-in-law, Nellie Phillips, opera-tor at the Sunset Telephone and Telegraph Company; and Mrs. Curtis' nephew, William Phillips, also a photoprinter. During the next seven years the fortunes of the Curtis and Phillips families were closely inter-twined, and the history of the Curtis studio was essentially a tale of these two families.

By 1897 the name Guptil was dropped and the firm became simply "Edward S. Curtis, Photographer and Photo-engraver."[2] During these last years of the nineteenth century, Curtis was working for the most part in portrait photography and photoengraving, but his interest in Northwest Coast Indians was developing.

2. In 1898 the Curtis photographic establishment was moved one block to the Downs Building on Second Avenue where it remained for more than sixteen years. It was this establishment that eventually came to be known officially as "The Curtis Studio." Asahel Curtis was now listed as a photographer instead of an engraver, and William Phillips had been promoted from photo-printer to photographer, probably a reflection of the increasing amount of time Edward Curtis was away from his studio.

4. *Curtis and Guptil advertisement,* Seattle City Directory, *1894–95. The spell-ing Guptill is apparently an error.*

In one interview made long after he was famous, Curtis claimed that his first Indian pictures were made at Tulalip on Puget Sound in 1896. In another interview he recalled that his first picture was of Princess Angeline, taken in Seattle. Princess Angeline was the aged daughter of Chief Sealth, a Suquamish Indian from whom the City of Seattle took its name. She made a meager living by gathering firewood and digging clams in the Seattle tidelands near her waterfront cabin. She died, ill and infirm, in May of 1896, so Curtis probably photographed her sometime in 1895 or early 1896.[3]

From his beginning collection of Indian portraits Curtis made exhibition prints of three studies, "The Clam Digger," "The Mussel Gatherer," and "Homeward," to enter in a contest sponsored by the National Photographic Convention. He was awarded a bronze medal and his pictures toured foreign countries, winning the admiration of audiences as well as the acclaim of critics. In this period Curtis was spending more time adventuring, taking pictures that pleased him, and making climbing trips on Mount Rainier, lugging with him a Premo dry-plate view camera.

The Harriman Alaska Expedition of 1899, of which Curtis was a member, was a major episode in his life and laid the foundation for his eventual meeting with President Roosevelt, and his financial sponsorship by John Pierpont Morgan for the American Indian project. He would not have been a member of the expedition were it not for an accidental meeting in the spring of 1898.

3. D. G. Inverarity, in a letter to his son, Robert Bruce Inverarity, wrote in 1947: "This takes me back to the Sunday afternoon when Ed. and I were out with Cameras, as usual, looking at the Indian Hop Pickers who were just beginning to come in near the old Yacht Club moorings. I saw an Indian in the bow of a canoe with siwashs making a bow on landing. . . . I took that picture which I called 'Tenas Canim' ["little canoe" in Chinook Jargon]. [This] was the first Indian picture that Curtis ever made and the beginning of his Indian collection." We do not know the title used by Curtis in his photograph of the same scene nor the date of this event, but it was prior to the Harriman Expedition of 1899 because Inverarity mentioned in this letter that the "Expedition put the finishing touch" on Curtis' interest in photographing Indians.

During one of his trips to Mount Rainier for the purpose of taking photographs, "he strayed," according to Andrews, "into the col below jagged Little Tahoma and there came upon a lost and despairing, half-starved climbing party. . . . Curtis learned after he got the men into his camp and thawed them out, that they were well-known scientists and government specialists—among them Dr. C. Hart Merriam, Chief of U.S. Biological Survey; Gifford Pinchot, Chief of U.S. Forestry Department and George Bird Grinnell, editor of Field and Stream Magazine. . . . Before the parties came down the mountain, Grinnell, Merriam, and Curtis became well acquainted and this friendship continued through correspondence after the editor and outdoorsman returned East" (1962:21). All of these men were people of prestige and power in government circles and in the community of natural scientists. Apparently Grinnell and Merriam were particularly impressed by Edward Curtis, and it was through Merriam that Curtis was invited to participate in the Harriman Expedition.

In the early spring of 1899 Edward H. Harriman was organizing an expedition to Alaska, in cooperation with the Washington Academy of Sciences. In planning the research work and selecting the personnel of the party, Harriman received the advice and assistance of Merriam. Merriam chose Edward Curtis as the photographer, and Curtis may have been able to choose his close friend D. G. Inverarity as his assistant. In any event Curtis and Inverarity were listed as the expedition photographers, although of these two only Curtis is given picture credits in the reports of the expedition.

The Harriman Expedition enabled Edward Curtis to associate with an illustrious and influential group of men. In addition to his new friends Merriam, Grinnell, and Pinchot, he met John Muir, William Healey Dall, John Burroughs, William H. Brewer, Frederick V. Coville, Daniel G. Elliot, A. K. Fisher, Henry Gannet, G. K. Gilbert, Charles A. Keeler, Trevor Kincaid, Robert Ridgeway, William E. Ritter, and William Trelease. Harriman had spared no expense. John Burroughs, one of the authors of the narrative of the Expedition, wrote, "We left New York on the afternoon of May 23, 1899, in a special train of palace cars, and took ship at Seattle the last day of the month." The Expedition sailed on the steamship "Geo. W. Elder," especially chartered for the purpose, and was gone just two months.

From a small house of hewn logs at Sidney on Puget Sound to the opulence of the Harriman Alaska Expedition with its wealthy patrons and famous men of science and letters, all in a period of eight years, must have made a profound impression on the mind of Edward Curtis, whose thirty-one years until this time had been spent in essentially rural and simple surroundings.

The Harriman Expedition was intellectually stimulating and physically exciting for Edward Curtis. He experienced a narrow escape while photographing the front of the giant glacier named for John Muir. Of this event Burroughs wrote, "One afternoon during our stay about half a mile of the front fell at once. The swell which it caused brought grief to our photographers who had ventured too near it. Their boat was filled and their plates were destroyed." In the report of the Expedition there is a photogravure of the front of Muir Glacier made from a photograph taken by Curtis just before the huge iceberg fell (Burroughs et al. 1901:facing p. 38). The wave almost swamped his canoe, and washed overboard a series of very large negatives of the glacier front. Besides the excitement of adventure the Harriman Expedition must have been the equivalent of a college education for Curtis. There was a perpetual combination of field exploration and scholarly lectures throughout the voyage (Burroughs et al. 1901:61–63). Teri McLuhan aptly called this expedition the "floating symposium" (Coleman and McLuhan 1972:ix).

With this exposure to other cultures, around the turn of the century Curtis had become obsessed with the idea that the American Indian was a vanishing race and that he, possessing the necessary skills and talent, was duty bound to produce a photographic record while it was still possible to do so. Curtis was not alone in this idea; in all likelihood he got it from George Bird Grinnell, with whom he spent time among the Blackfeet Indians in Montana. Curtis was wrong about the vanishing race. The Indians were increasing in population and were destined to increase even more in the twentieth century. But he was right in believing that the old traditional cultures were changing and might well be lost to posterity if he did not record them in picture and word. Accordingly he persevered in his goal to produce an accurate record of American Indians as they were before the non-Indians conquered them and took away their lands in the name of Christianity and civilization.

Curtis was fortunate to work at a time when he could obtain this record: there were always available older people who knew the traditional ways and would cooperate with him in producing his images. They would willingly don old-style costumes and demonstrate old-style artifacts when these were no longer in use. But the important thing was that the Indians at this time still knew the old ways even if they were no longer practiced, and were able to provide an accurate cultural reconstruction.

His work took Curtis to the southwestern United States in 1903 to photograph the Mojave, Zuni, and Apache Indians, and he exhibited about fifty of the portraits from this expedition in his studio. With Curtis away from Seattle much of the time the photographic establishment had been run at various times by his brother Asahel and members of the Phillips family. Times were changing, however, and Adolph F. Muhr ran the studio from 1904 until his death in 1913. He was the first operator who was neither a Curtis nor an in-law.

Before joining Curtis, Muhr had worked as a photographer in Omaha, Nebraska. In 1898 he took the pictures of Indians attending the United States Indian Congress of the Trans-Mississippi and International Exposition held in Omaha, although these photographs were copyrighted by F. A. Rinehart, the official photographer for the Exposition. Muhr made more than a thousand images of Indians representing thirty-six different tribes and wrote the captions for each picture according to a small printed catalogue in the archives of the Burke Museum, entitled "Rineharts Platinum Prints of American Indians." This document contains an introduction by A. F. Muhr:

At the United States Indian Congress of the Trans-Mississippi and International Exposition at Omaha, 1898, were gathered upward of five hundred Indians, under the direction of Capt. W. A. Mercer, U.S.A. delegations, and individual types of thirty-six tribes, who formerly traversed the vast plains between the Mississippi and the Rocky Mountains, where they hunted the buffalo, made war on the intruding whites or on each other. Here was afforded an opportunity for them to meet on neutral ground, bury the tomahawk, and smoke the pipe of peace. They also met the white man in greater numbers, and on a footing which could not help but promote a better feeling and understanding.

Being employed by Mr. Rinehart, the official photographer, the writer was assigned the task of photographing the Indians, into which he carried the zest of a novel experience. They were timid at first, hung back like children, but a little coaxing and a better acquaintance soon made smooth sailing.

When he took over the Curtis studio Muhr was completely responsible for its operation and management. The photographs taken in the field by Curtis were sent to the studio where they were processed by Muhr and his assistants. One of those assistants was the photographer Imogen Cunningham, who was employed as a printer in the studio in 1907 and 1908, and who later acknowledged Muhr's strong influence on her work. Curtis praises Muhr in his introduction to the first nine volumes of *The North American Indian*, and Muhr wrote a tribute to Curtis, entitled "E. S. Curtis and His Work," published in *Photo-Era* magazine (July 1907). It seems appropriate to let Adolph Muhr speak for himself, and his article is quoted here at some length:

Curtis himself is the most tireless worker that I have ever known, and his example is so contagious that every one connected with him seems fired by the same enthusiasm and imbued with the same energy and ambition to do things and accomplish the work laid out for him.

We have seen very little of Mr. Curtis at the Seattle Studio, especially in the last two years, his time being taken up almost entirely by his work in the field, where he is busy with camera and note-book, gathering material. The short intervals at home are devoted to writing up the field notes and the preparation of the MSS, for the forthcoming publication, "The Indians of North America." This publication will be as elaborate and important an undertaking as any ever attempted, and will, for boldness, be a close rival to that of Audubon, nearly a century ago. . . .

Although Mr. Curtis is one of the most genial and pleasant of men, he is extremely modest and reticent in regard to his personal experiences; he shuns notoriety. It is only when some requisition necessitates an explanation that we get any information of the numerous accidents and mishaps which are the outcome of the strenuous life which he leads in the field. . . . he is naturally equipped to grapple with a subject that would tax another's patience to the utmost or compel the entire abandonment of the project. Sitting up at night to repair an outfit by candlelight, that might seem worse than useless is evidence of the sincerity of purpose and absolute determination to carry on the work in spite of all obstacles. . . .

On one trip he was confronted by a roaring torrent where a dry aroya was expected. He hastily converted the canvas wagon-covers into bateaux and floated the outfit across. On another occasion he risked his life to recover his outfit, that was spilled from the wagon in fording a stream. . . .

These [inconveniences] Mr. Curtis considers lightly, and nothing compared to the difficulty he meets in his dealings with that unknown quality—the Indian. The qualities so necessary to success in dealing with him, Mr. Curtis possesses to a remarkable degree: tact, diplomacy, and courage, which, combined with a good stock of patience and perseverence, have made it possible to succeed where others have failed. The Indian quite naturally is suspicious and distrustful of advances made by his white brothers. . . .

There have been times when he seemed an unwelcome spectator and marked hostility was manifested, when diplomacy was of no avail, and only by an exhibition of that unflinching courage, not yielding the least ground, he not only conquered the belligerent spirits, but won them as friends. Nothing appeals so strongly to an Indian, in whom the savage instinct is always dormant, as a brave and courageous act.

During last season's work Mr. Curtis was initiated into the sacred mysteries of the rites of the Snake Priests of the Hopis. This could be done only by adoption, and he is now a son of these quaint people. He lived among them during the Nine Days' Ceremony; went with them on their quests for snakes, and to find whether his heart was good, each snake, when found, whether Bull Snake, Blue Racer or Rattler, was hung around his neck. If the heart is not good the snake will bite, and as he came back to tell his experience, his heart must be good.

Muhr's account of Edward Curtis is particularly complimentary, considering that Muhr himself was an accomplished photographer who had photographed hundreds of Indians.

During most of 1905 Curtis was with his field party in the Southwest. Of this he wrote: "During the spring, summer, autumn and the first half of winter, we worked with the Apache, Navajo, Jicarilla, Apache, Hopi, Pima, Papago, Havasupai, Qahatika, Yuma and Mohave. . . . Our object was to complete the research for the first two volumes and every member of our party worked to the limit of his physical strength to that end. At the close of the field work our main party of three men and a stenographer settled down in obscure rooms to do the final work of getting those two volumes ready for publication. This consumed about ninety days and during all that time we all slept and took our meals at the rooms, in order to have no interruptions" (quoted in Ewing 1972:87). Only once was Curtis accompanied to the field by his wife and children. In 1906 Clara, a son, and two daughters traveled by train from Seattle to Los Angeles and then on to Gallup, New Mexico, where Edward met them. From Gallup they all went by wagon to Canon de Chelly on the Navajo reservation. Except for this sojourn, Curtis was away from home and his wife for much of his married life.

Professionally, these were particularly active and rewarding years. In the Northwest, as well as in the eastern United States, he gave illustrated lectures using colored lantern slides that Adolph Muhr made from his negatives. In 1905 and again in 1906 he spoke to members of the National Geographic Society in Washington, D.C., and he was then also having successful exhibitions in New York, Washington, Boston, and Pittsburgh. Through C. Hart Merriam and Mr. and Mrs. Edward Harriman, Edward Curtis and his work were brought to the attention of President Theodore Roosevelt, who quickly became a fan. In fact, Roosevelt was such an admirer of Curtis that he obtained his services as the official and only photographer present at the wedding of Alice Roosevelt to Nicholas M. Longworth in Washington in 1906.

William E. Myers, a former reporter for the Seattle *Daily Star*, became the newest member of Curtis' team, and contributed significantly to the North American Indian project. Curtis' regard for Myers is best expressed by Curtis: "He joined me in the field in 1906, while research among the Navajo was in progress, and thereafter we spent practically every season in camp together until the close of 1925. His service during that time has been able, faithful, and self-sacrificing, often in the face of adverse conditions, hardship, and discouragement" (1928:xii). Myers is acknowledged in eighteen of the twenty volumes of *The North American Indian*, and in four of these, he receives the only acknowledgment.

Andrews quotes another tribute to Myers by Curtis:

[Myers] was a rapid shorthand writer, a speedy typist who had majored in English literature and had developed an uncanny ear for phonetics. In spelling he was a second Webster.

To the Indians his skill in phonetics was awesome magic. An old informant would pronounce a seven syllable word and Myers would repeat it without a second's hesitation, which to the old Indian was awe-inspiring—as it was to me. At most times while extracting information, Myers sat on my left and the interpreter on my right. I led in asking questions, Myers and the interpreter prompted me if I overlooked any important points. What chance did the poor old Indian have when confronted by such a combination? By writing all information in shorthand we speeded the work to the utmost. Our trio could do more work in a year than a lone investigator, writing in longhand, and lacking phonetic skill, could do in five years. That is why we did so much in the time we had. Also we knew nothing of labor unions in our party. Myers neatly typed his day's collection before going to bed. In that way field notes were kept up to the minute. Our average working time for a six months' season would exceed sixteen hours a day [Andrews 1962:44].

The work on the volumes proceeded in a small log cabin in the mountains of Montana. "Our breakfast hour was 7:30, beginning active work at 9:00; a half hour for lunch and an hour for supper: and we then worked until 1 A.M. This was done every day of the month until spring. I did not take a day off during that time, the only interruption being a single trip to the post-office, six miles away. I permitted mail to come to our camp but once a week and no newspapers were allowed. Every thought and every moment had to be given to the work" (Curtis quoted in Ewing 1972:87).

III. The Motion Picture Years: 1910–14

About 1910 Edward Curtis had the idea of making a full-length motion picture on a commercial basis. Prior to this time, probably as early as 1906, he had used motion picture photography to record special events and ceremonies. He was now thinking of producing a feature film, in addition to all of his regular work on the Indian project. In this five-year period Curtis had become increasingly occupied by financial affairs and lecture tours and as a consequence his two chief associates, William Myers and Edmund Schwinke, frequently undertook the photography, fieldwork, and writing of manuscripts on their own.

Edmund August Schwinke joined Curtis and Myers in January 1910 and immediately was in the thick of things. According to his notes (in the Burke Museum archives), he joined Curtis, Myers, and a cook at the Curtis cabin on Puget Sound near Port Orchard, where they worked on volumes 5, 6, and 7 of *The North American Indian*.[1] In June they made a trip by boat down the Columbia River from Pasco to Astoria and the river mouth to work with nearby Indians in Oregon and Washington. Next they traveled over the wagon road to the lands of the Quinault.

1. In 1901–2, according to records at the Kitsap County Auditor's Office, Curtis sold some of the homestead and brickyard at Sidney to the Port Orchard Clay Company, sold much of the machinery to Mitchell, Lewis, and Staves, and mortgaged various properties. He kept the family land located on Rich Passage in the Wautauga Beach area and a few years later his father-in-law built a summer home for the Curtis family. Curtis' daughter, Florence, describes the retreat: "That was a beautiful 50 acres and I knew it from one end to the other, as well as the great tides that sweep through the Narrows. Nestled among madrona and fir trees, burlaped walls covered with Indian pictures, burden baskets filled with huckleberry branches, Indian rugs on the floor. . . . Dad also used the cabin one year or winter to work with his crew on *The North American Indian*" (letter, 13 February 1975).

After returning to Seattle, where Curtis purchased a forty-foot boat equipped with sails and engine, they went to Alert Bay and the Kwakiutl country of northern Vancouver Island to begin preparations for the motion picture.

Curtis described the field work of this year as a "season of hard effort with good results. The work was particularly hard for me as I had to handle my own boat, do my own work in regular picture making, collecting; and to add further to my task, I found long before the end of the season that money was so scarce that I could not afford a cook, so I sent the cook home and did that part of the work myself. Our breakfast hour was usually 4:00 and supper 8:00 to 10:00. My working hours for the season were scarcely short of twenty hours a day" (Ewing 1972:87–88).

During the winter of 1910–11, however, he was involved largely in a "bookselling effort," because the five years of research supported by J. Pierpont Morgan had come to an end. He adds: "I did, however, manage to keep Myers and Schwinke at work in a half supported sort of way. Myers, in addition to a fairly successful piece of work in British Columbia did six months of most successful work in the Hopi country; but I personally, had only a few short weeks in camp" (Ewing 1972:88).

Curtis was in New York with Schwinke for the first five months of 1911. Myers worked with the Indians of Vancouver Island that summer, and Schwinke may have been working alone with the Makah Indians at Neah Bay and Cape Flattery, since in his acknowledgments to volume 11 of *The North American Indian* Curtis gives Schwinke credit for collecting the Makah ethnographic data. In the autumn, Curtis and Schwinke were back in New York and Curtis continued his lecture series to raise funds and advertise *The North American Indian*.

"The winter of 1911–12," according to Curtis, "was somewhat a repetition of the former one. At the end of June, I gave up the effort for further money and went west and at once into camp, inadequately outfitted and short of funds to do efficient work; the small amount used being in fact available through a second mortgage on my home. Desiring to accomplish all possible on our limited money, I took no camp-cook, but did all that myself, in addition to my other work. This again meant a season of twenty hours a day" (Ewing 1972:88).

In January of 1912 Curtis and Schwinke were in Reading, Pennsylvania. Newspaper accounts provide a good description of Curtis' lecture on "The Vanishing Race":

> For two hours a gathering of nearly 1,000 people . . . were held spellbound . . . by the vividly realistic presentation of the Life of the North American Indian by Edward S. Curtis. . . . The preliminary talk was prefaced with a prelude by the orchestra, "The Spirit of the Indian Life," a characteristic outburst of strangely harmonious sound, vibrant with the unbridled primitive impulses of the native Americans. The wonderful interpretation was given a great hand.
>
> It can be better understood when it is explained that Mr. Curtis gathered the music by means of phonographs and had it transposed by Henry F. Gilbert, of Boston, the orchestra leader. By faithful practice the sounds of the Indian musicians were perfectly mimiced.
>
> The pictures themselves, both the stereopticon and the cinemateographic were superb masterpieces of the photographer's art. The stereoptican views were colored true to nature, showing scenes . . . that defy description. The beautiful language employed by Mr. Curtis in explaining each picture lent a refining touch to the occasion.

Edmund Schwinke and Edward Curtis were in the East until July of 1912 when they returned to Seattle from New York City. Late that summer Curtis, Myers, and Schwinke were on Vancouver Island, working with Nootka and Kwakiutl Indians, and also visiting the whaling factory at Sechart on the west coast.

Schwinke had become increasingly important in Curtis' business affairs, which were certainly entangled at times. Some documents from the Burke Museum archives illustrate the problems. A promissory note for one hundred dollars, issued in New York City on 17 June 1912, to the order of Edmund Schwinke and payable on demand at the office of the North American Indian, was signed by R. H. Schumacher, a man of mystery and apparently a rogue, who was selling subscriptions for Curtis in Paris. There were other such promissory notes, as evidenced by Schwinke's letter of 24 July 1912, to Lewis Albert, who was in charge of financial affairs at the New York office of the North American Indian.

Dear Albert: I enclose Schumacher's note to me for $53.75, the money I loaned him. (I can imagine you saying things about my qualifications as an easy mark, but it is done). You may handle this the same way you will other I.O.U.s of his when some money comes in, if it ever does.

When you write me about this, better address me at the Hotel Avondale. They will take care of it, and I will be certain it won't get into the chief's hands. He often opens your mail to me. He probably wouldn't if it was marked personal, but he would begin to wonder what it was about. Sincerely yours,[2]

On 4 February 1913, Albert wrote:

My dear Schwinke: Mr. Curtis has asked that I write you to ascertain the initials of Mr. Chapin of the San Francisco *Call*.

Further, for my record will you kindly give me an estimate as to the number and copies of volumes and folios of No. IX we've ordered. I want to keep up my check on Blackwell.

I dislike very much to mention the fact but I am afraid our friend Schumacher is a bad egg; not entirely will I say from choice or desire, but rather

2. Only the carbons of a number of Schwinke's letters are now available in the Burke Museum archives.

because it is so much easier for him to borrow money than to work for it. I have never before had a chance to drop you a little note on this matter for the reason that I did not care to have it go into the hands of the Chief. Now, what I would suggest doing is that you write [Schumacher] a letter (his address and the only one I have ever had is c/o United States Express Co., Paris, France) making your case as beseeching as possible and telling him how much you need the money, etc., etc. He has some little regard for you, I know, and this appeal may bring some result. You might also mention to him that his actions abroad have put me in rather hot water. He may rejoice at this, on account of the way I have now put my foot down on him, or else his further pity (if he has any) might be aroused. I really do not think he is bad at heart. He has pawned or pledged for security some of the pictures loaned him and one can only surmise what else he might have done on the other side. He has never gotten any further than Paris and judging from one or two of his letters to me I am afraid the women there were too much for him.

I do not know what arrangement Mr. Curtis and yourself have made regarding checks issued by him [Curtis], but for your information, as far as I know, one was issued No. 399, dated January 28th, in favor of John Andrew & Son on the Harriman Bank for $700.00. I further issued a note at four months, dated February 1st, payable to John Andrew & Son, for $751.50. I also issued a check for $36.50 in favor of Jacob Reed's Sons, Phila., account of H.P.C. [Harold Curtis, son of E. S. Curtis].

With very kind regards and best wishes, I am Very sincerely yours, Lewis Albert.

P.S. Don't forget about writing Schumacher and throwing aside all modesty. This, if anything, may be the means of getting something from him.

We cannot tell whether Schwinke ever got his money back, or, for that matter, what Schumacher was up to. We do, however, have an undated letter from Curtis at the Cosmos Club in Washington, D.C., to Schwinke, indicating Curtis' suspicions of Schumacher's activities. "The wire from Mr. Marshall causes me to do some thinking. Why did the letters not reach me. Can it be possible that through such letters Schumacher got the thoughts of Hamptons and that the letters from Marshall were held up. Keep your eyes open. I am doing some good work here and expect to be in N.Y. on Monday." (Edward

Marshall had interviewed Curtis for *Hampton Magazine* in an article entitled "The Vanishing Red Man," and had remained in touch with Curtis regarding possible stories for the publication.)

Curtis remained in the East for most of 1913, organizing and funding his local firm company. Adolph Muhr died in that year, leaving Ella McBride (who had joined the Studio in 1911) and Edward's daughter, Beth, in charge of operations, probably with some help from Schwinke. Meanwhile, Myers was gathering ethnographic material for the book in northern British Columbia. His letter to Schwinke on 14 June points to the increased responsibilities Curtis was delegating to his two assistants.

Dear Schwinke, I am leaving Cape Mudge for Rivers Inlet—Address Beaver, B.C.—where doubtless I shall be when you come up, as [George] Hunt says we shall find several tribes there.

I have with me both vols. of the Handbook, Boas, and my Kwakiutl Ms., my tent and floor cloth, bedding and cot, and typewriter. Unless we are going to live aboard ship, you had better leave your machine. Hunt has the phonograph here, but we shall need records.

Following are some wants of Hunt: the old white one-pole tent (unless we have our own cruiser to live in); some small clips or wire springs to be used for catching the skin and pulling it away from the flesh, as if a thong had been inserted in the flesh (the cedar rope will be attached to the clip and conceal the metal); a camera to take a picture about 10×12, of a grade comparable to the one he now has, a 5×7 costing $17.50. Or if the chief thinks it would be better for him to use his 5×7 and enlarge to 10×12, get him the necessary apparatus for the process.

Your Maka [sic] notes from page 106 to the end came a few days since, but 1 to 105 I have not seen. Better have them traced.

Some pretty good material has turned up since my letter to the chief, especially the war stories. These fellows were the champion murderers and pirates of the coast. Yours, W. E. Myers.

This letter indicates that Myers and George Hunt were collecting ethnographic data and that Hunt was doing the photography. Moreover, they were planning to stage a scene for still photography in which Indians would appear to be suspended on cedar ropes attached to thongs inserted through their flesh. Such photographs do not appear in volume 10 of *The North American Indian*, but the following summer such a scene was filmed for *In the Land of the Head-Hunters*.[3]

Schwinke and Curtis did not go north to join Myers and Hunt until late summer. We have a fragment of a letter written by Schwinke that only fits the 1913 schedule. He wrote, "This time we are going up along the Coast of British Columbia to do a moving picture thing of the Indians. I am glad we are about ready to leave, as the summer so far has been very discouraging. I have certainly been busy the past week getting things together for the trip."

In September and October of 1913, Curtis, Myers, and Schwinke were on Vancouver Island working on Kwakiutl ethnography and, simultaneously, the documentary motion picture that was finally filmed the following spring and summer. That Schwinke was kept busy after his return to Seattle is made manifest in a fragment of a letter written by him on 25 December 1913: "Had a very nice time at the Curtises last night, but I drew a blank on Christmas dinners for today. However, I don't mind it so much, because I haven't had any Sundays lately and very little rest at other times, and it's great just to loaf. . . . I must tell you that I am learning to tango. Have had five lessons, and think I'm doing fairly well. 'Everybody's doin' it,' so there was nothing to do but to get into line. I read in today's paper that the Tango has reached Tanana."

On at least two counts, 1914 was a memorable year. Edward Curtis was elected an honorary member of the University of Washington chapter of Phi Beta Kappa, in recognition of his considerable achievements as

---

3. George Hunt is best known for the help he gave the anthropologist Franz Boas, supplying Boas with virtually all of his material on Kwakiutl ethnography, folklore, and linguistics. Hunt also supplied Curtis and Myers with much of their information and handled all the local arrangements for the motion picture. He was involved with Curtis' movie from 1911 through 1914.

ethnographer and author. He also finished *In the Land of the Head-Hunters*. Curtis, Schwinke, and Myers spent May, June, and July at various locations among Kwakiutl Indians at the northern end of Vancouver Island. They filmed the scenes and people with a motion picture camera and a still camera. Schwinke with his own Kodak took a number of still shots, some of which we have used in this book. The film taken with the motion picture camera became *In the Land of the Head-Hunters* and the Curtis stills became illustrations for volume 10 of *The North American Indian*. The motion picture was processed and a print, hand-toned in suitable colors, was ready for presentation to audiences in New York and Seattle in the late autumn of 1914.

We have previously mentioned that Robert Flaherty's film, *Nanook of the North*, was conceptually similar to Curtis' film in its reconstruction of an earlier phase of aboriginal culture. Although Curtis had been taking motion pictures since 1906 and had been planning his full-length documentary since 1910, there is a coincidental overlap between him and Flaherty in 1913 and 1914. It seems remarkable that two persons were independently planning the same kind of film with the same kinds of inherent problems and using similar approaches to achieve their goals.

In 1913 Curtis was well along with his preparations for filming, whereas Flaherty was just beginning, as he indicates: "On my third expedition into the north in 1913 . . . I included in my equipment all the necessary apparatus for making a motion picture film of the Eskimos" (Flaherty 1924:119). Flaherty began filming on Baffin Island in February 1914, focusing on the Eskimos building igloos, sledging with dog teams, hunting seals, and performing conjuring dances. His last segment was a caribou hunt for which he mounted camera and tripod on a dog sled and filmed the hunt from his sled pulled by "galloping dogs." In the autumn of 1914 he returned to Toronto after editing the film, of which he wrote: "It was too crude to be interesting" (ibid.:26).

Thus Flaherty was still learning the use of the motion picture camera in 1914, the year that Curtis filmed and released his own picture. We had a strong intuition that Robert Flaherty had seen Edward Curtis' motion picture. We knew that Flaherty had returned to Toronto in the autumn and winter of 1914–15, which was when *In the Land of the Head-Hunters* was being shown in New York. Moreover, the long, rave review of the Curtis film by W. Stephen Bush (see chap. 1) could have been known to Flaherty, as could have Vachel Lindsay's praise of Curtis in *The Art of the Moving Picture*.

In the late spring of 1979 we learned that Flaherty had indeed seen *In the Land of the Head-Hunters* at a special viewing in Curtis' headquarters in New York. According to Professor Jay Ruby, of Temple University's Department of Anthropology (personal communication), Flaherty's wife Frances kept a diary. On Friday, 9 April 1915, according to her record, she and Robert Flaherty visited the Curtis Studio. Although they did not meet Curtis they were shown the portfolio of photogravures associated with the Kwakiutl volume and were told about Curtis' motion picture. On Monday Flaherty met Curtis by appointment and they made plans to screen the Curtis film and Flaherty's Baffin Island Eskimo footage. This they did on Tuesday morning, 13 April 1915, before a small select audience. Afterwards Curtis and the Flahertys had lunch together and Curtis gave them "the benefit of his own experience in the moving picture world."

Equipped with his new knowledge, Robert Flaherty went north again in the summer of 1915 determined to make a better movie of Eskimos. This time he was on the Belcher Islands in Hudson's Bay. During the late winter and spring of 1916 he made his second movie, which was a great improvement over his first. He made the disastrous mistake of smoking a cigarette while editing nitrate film and "the last inch of it went up in smoke" (Flaherty 1924:133).

Despite his loss Flaherty was determined to make his motion picture of the Eskimos. Financed by the Revillon Frères fur trading company he returned to the north in 1921 wholly for the purpose of making a motion picture. Flaherty arrived at the Revillon Frères post at Cape Dufferin in northeastern Hudson's Bay in mid-August of 1921. "Of the Eskimos who were known to the post," said Flaherty, "a dozen all told were selected for the film" (ibid.:133). He put the women to work making traditional clothing of caribou skin. Surely influenced by Curtis, Flaherty wanted to show only the old-time culture as it was before the white men came and he did not want his actors' Scottish woolen clothing to destroy the mood.

He first filmed the walrus hunting scene, which was similar to the one he had made five years earlier and lost by fire. Then he had his actors construct a snow house large enough for the filming of interior scenes. When the roof was cut away so that there would be enough light for his Akeley motion picture camera, Flaherty noted, "Nanook and his family went to sleep and awakened with all the cold of out-of-doors pouring in" (ibid.:140). In July of 1922 Flaherty used up the last of his film on a most successful whale hunting scene in which his people harpooned and killed five white whales. Then in August he returned to Toronto and put together his *Nanook of the North*. The rest is film history.

We believe that the Curtis influence on Robert Flaherty is manifested in a number of ways after their New York meeting. Prior to that time Flaherty's motion picture was something of a travelogue and, by his own term, "crude." In his 1921–22 film Flaherty, like Curtis, wanted to portray the culture as it was before Europeans influenced it. Like Curtis he hired a select group of actors and people to make traditional clothing. He eliminated tools, weapons, and utensils of the white man and constructed a false snowhouse for his interior scenes.

In the next three chapters we will show how Curtis in 1914 made his motion picture in much the same manner as Flaherty did eight years later.

IV. Curtis and the Kwakiutl

Of all these coast-dwellers the Kwakiutl tribes were one of the most important groups, and at the present time theirs are the only villages where primitive life can still be observed. Their ceremonies are developed to a point which fully justifies the term dramatic. They are rich in mythology and tradition. Their sea-going canoes possess the most beautiful lines, and few tribes have built canoes approaching theirs in size. Their houses are large, and skillfully constructed. Their heraldic columns evidence considerable skill in carving, though not equalling those of the Haida and Tsimshian, from whom this phase of their art probably was borrowed. In their development of ceremonial masks and costumes they are far in advance of any other group of North American Indians.

With these words in the introduction to volume 10 of his monumental work, *The North American Indian*, Edward Curtis indicated the reasons why he spent parts of five seasons gathering material on the Kwakiutl, why the Kwakiutl volume has more pages (on thinner paper) than any of the other nineteen, and why he made his dramatic motion picture, *In the Land of the Head-Hunters*, among the Kwakiutl.

In 1914—the year in which both volume 10 and the film were finished—the Kwakiutl were living a life which was far removed in many ways from that which Curtis portrayed. His claim that "primitive life can still be observed" in the Kwakiutl villages was true only in part. The Kwakiutl had had almost constant contact with white men—explorers, traders, missionaries, school teachers, loggers, fishermen, businessmen, and government agents—since June of 1792 when in the space of a few days surveying expeditions from England and Spain and a Bengal-based trading ship threaded their ways through the channels of the Kwakiutl country. In Curtis' time no Kwakiutl man or woman habitu-ally wore true native dress, although the trade blanket was commonly worn as an outer garment by old people. Most of the houses of the area were of the old native type, although many had glass-paned windows and front walls of milled lumber. Dugout canoes were all but gone; planked sailboats and a few gas- and steam-driven vessels had almost entirely supplanted them for fishing and travel. The famous anthropologist Franz Boas had already been studying and recording Kwakiutl customs and language for twenty-eight years.

Curtis was correct in the sense that, in spite of over a century of white contact, the Kwakiutl had retained a remarkable amount of their traditional culture. Native foods were still staple, the potlatch and associated ceremonial activities (despite a ban by the government) were at their height, and the whole fabric of traditional social organization and attitudes was intact. In contrast to the situation in many other parts of the Pacific Coast, Kwakiutl art, motivated by the lively ceremonial activity, was still going strong. The masks and costumes which excited Curtis were a vital part of the Kwakiutl scene.

Edward Curtis gave full credit to his chief informant and interpreter, George Hunt. It is fair to say that without Hunt's assistance Curtis would certainly have had a much more difficult time in amassing his Kwakiutl information. His success, as that of Franz Boas, Adrian Jacobsen (who was collecting for the German museums in the early 1880s), and anthropologist Samuel Barrett of the Milwaukee Public Museum, *all hinged* on the knowledge and cooperation of this one man. Each of them credited his assistance. We would go so far as to say that it is unlikely that Edward Curtis would have successfully completed his motion picture without the help of George Hunt.

When Curtis came to the Kwakiutl country he had already finished his work among tribes whose names conjured up the most romantic images: the Navajo and Apache of the Southwest; the Western Sioux, Crow, Cheyenne, and Piegan of the Great Plains; and the Nez Perce and other tribes of the Plateau. He had interviewed and photographed Chief Joseph and Geronimo and the warriors who had followed them, as well as Crow and Arikara who had scouted for Custer, and the Sioux and Cheyenne who had fought and defeated him.

Probably the idea of making moving picture records of American Indian cultures came to him during these experiences. We know he had been using a motion picture camera off and on since 1906. But it was during the time spent with the Kwakiutl in 1911–12 that his grand plan was born. And his epic documentary *In the Land of the Head-Hunters* was the only feature-length film he ever made.

The Continental Film Company

At the time Curtis began to formulate his plan to make motion pictures they were at the peak of a wave of popularity. Films with Indian themes were particularly successful, and Curtis must have considered his background in the subject and his photographic skills to be made to order for taking advantage of this potential bonanza. He also deplored the quality of the usual commercial article: artificial plot, costumes and props that were mismatched or outright fakes, and inaccurate portrayals of native customs by made-up, non-Indian actors. He saw his planned motion pictures as being both financially rewarding and educational.

In an effort to obtain support for his film project Curtis wrote a letter dated 2 May 1912 to Dr. Charles D. Walcott, Secretary of the Smithsonian Institution (Jay Ruby 1979, personal communication). That letter contained a short proposal outlining a rough plan for a film about Kwakiutl life. Although we had obtained a copy of this proposal in 1975 we were uncertain of the date. It seems likely that identical letters were sent to other potential supporters in 1912.

It has been suggested that I make, in connection with my photographic field work, a complete series of motion pictures of the most important tribes, such pictures illustrating, so far as possible, the activities of their lives, particularly domestic and ceremonial, not carelessly caught fragments of superficial, indifferent matter, but rather carefully studied and worked out subjects, in order that every picture be an unquestioned document.

Such pictures would require the utmost care in costuming. As an illustration, if a certain ceremonial was to be pictured, and of fifty actors ten had correct costumes, and the other forty modern or mongrel ones, it would be necessary to secure or have made the forty additional correct costumes. Further, a broad knowledge of the subject would necessarily be required at all times, to make certain that ceremonies, dancers, and other activities be indigenous to the tribe treated, and not borrowed, or, if borrowed, that the fact be clearly set forth in the picture. My effort would be to go back as close to the primal life as possible, illustrating my thoughts in this respect. Let us presume to be making a picture of the natives of the British Columbia coast tribes. Theirs was a populous region, the people proud, vigorous, crafty, cruel, constantly engaged in warfare, and depending mainly on the sea for food. Their ceremonial life had reached an important stage of development. As artisans they possessed considerable skill, felling the giant cedars of the forest and making from them ocean-going canoes, carving and decorating the well-known totem poles and house posts. Their ceremonial masks are in decoration and variety scarcely surpassed. In weaving they were very skillful. Pictures should be made to illustrate the period before the white man came, keeping in mind all their activities. The following are some of the activities which should be pictured:

Making stone implements, men in loin-cloths. Felling giant cedars with stone tools, and splitting them into planks. Cutting planks from living trees. Making a canoe, carrying it from the forest to the water's edge. Carving a totem pole, and erecting and dedicating it; this is a ceremonial occasion. Constructing one of their great ceremonial houses; carving and placing the four wonderful house posts; raising the timbers supporting the roof (these are sometimes eighty feet in length and two feet in diameter); building one of these houses was a great event which could be likened to a festival, bringing into the picture not only workers in loin-cloths, but important men and women in their gala costumes. Carving their remarkable masks, and carving and decorating the wooden chests. Women gathering cedarbark (this is used for making the greater part of their clothing), working the bark, and weaving into cloth and mats. Weaving woolen blankets (mountain-goat wool). Men and women taking and preparing the different varieties of fish, digging clams, and gathering the many varieties of shellfish. The picturesque capture of a devil-fish (this was and is a food delicacy). Porpoise spearing. A whaling expedition; ceremonial preparation; party starting on the expedition; killing the whale, return to the village; ceremonial attending the bringing in of the whale. (The whale ceremony is most important one.) Ceremonial preparation for a war expedition (all such expeditions are by canoe); return of the war party; ceremony of victory; burial of the dead. (Bodies are placed in carved chests or in canoes, and then lifted high into trees and fastened there.) Burial party taking the body to some island of the dead (this is a fleet of canoes). The Potlatch or gift ceremony. The important winter ceremony or dance (this includes many beautiful masked dancers). The devotional life. The wedding and its attendant picturesque ceremonies.

A picture as outlined would literally show all the important activities, and would be of inestimable value if properly done. If carelessly attempted I would consider it a calamity [Burke Museum archives].

His plan was grand, but before he finished his film he had eliminated much of the detail of everyday life and activities, and concentrated on war, adventure, and ceremonial life. In doing this, however, Curtis gave it consistency and saved it from being an overly long ethnographic record. We wish he had made two films.

To implement his plan Curtis organized the Continental Film Company, with himself as president and treasurer, Willis B. Herr as secretary, and four other trustees: C. H. Clark, E. L. Grondahl, C. H. Cobb, and F. W. Baker. He proposed making a series of pictures to cover "all the tribes of America, both North and South" (see Appendix 1). The futility of this plan is emphasized by the fact that his great life's work, the twenty-volume *North American Indian*, covered actually only a handful of the tribes of western North America. He also suffered from an acute dose of wishful thinking in suggesting that each of his pictures, if moderately successful, should pay a minimum profit of $100,000 for the first year, and that they would continue paying dividends for years to come. In fact he completed only one picture (and that one much less pretentious than his glowing plan), which soon slipped into obscurity and lay virtually unknown for sixty years.

Making the Film

Although Curtis has written that he spent parts of five seasons, from 1910 to 1914, working with the Kwakiutl, we could find no direct record of when he actually began making the film. By comparing the various scenarios and shooting scripts with the film and with his finished volume on the Kwakiutl, we had attempted to reconstruct a rough schedule. Then, in the space of a few months, two remarkable and hitherto unknown sources of information on the subject came to light. Both greatly enlarged our knowledge of the making of the film, and each clarified much of the sequence of events.

The first was the discovery, in early 1977, of photographs made by Edmund Schwinke during the filming. Through the efforts of Mick Gidley, who had located the photographs, and the cooperation of Mrs. Schwinke, both the photographs and the relevant correspondence were obtained by the Burke Museum. The Schwinke photographs shed a great deal of light on the actual making of Curtis' film. They help to explain some of the techniques used and to clarify George Hunt's role in the project. In addition to this pictorial information, they contain a major clue to the chronology of the filming. Schwinke numbered the photographs, and his numbering system records the month and year of the exposure. All of his photographs taken during the actual filming of the motion picture were made during May, June and July of 1914, and most of these are dated in June. The second discovery, discussed in chapter 5, was George Hunt's ledger of his work for Curtis.

In an article published in 1915 in *Strand Magazine* Curtis was quoted as saying he had met George Hunt "several years" before starting the film, when he had been studying and photographing the Kwakiutl, indicating that the movie was made toward the end of his Kwakiutl work. His first stay with the Kwakiutl was probably taken up with the business of establishing contacts and credibility. Some still photography was done as early as 1912, according to Schwinke's photograph numbers (figs. 5 and 6), although many of the most spectacular plates in volume 10 were photographed in conjunction with the film. The extent of this earlier work is made apparent by the descriptions in the proposal quoted on page 32. The photographs and proposal show an understanding of Kwakiutl life and a familiarity with the local scene which came from the time Curtis spent with these people, and they clearly precede the filming since very few of the scenes proposed were actually included. The proposal has the quality of a rough preliminary scenario—an exploration of the possibilities.

Upon his introduction to Kwakiutl culture, with George Hunt's help Curtis and his assistant Myers began recording information on native customs. The richness of Kwakiutl tradition in art and ceremony, captured so well in his photographs, excited in him the thought of making a motion picture, which must have seemed the best means of preserving in detail the way of life that he saw disappearing around him. Always the artist, Curtis would never have been satisfied with a true documentary record on film. He believed, and not without reason, that the action had to be staged to capture the powerfully dramatic character of the people and their lives. Since in his pictures he always, by his own state-

5. *In September of 1912, Curtis photographed a Nákwakhdakhw chief at Blunden Harbour. In order to include in his photograph the entire painted screen hanging on the house, it was necessary to build a platform for the photographer and camera, since the houses of Blunden Harbour (and of most Kwakiutl villages) were close to the high bank of the beach. The "street" in front of the houses of Blunden Harbour is a boardwalk supported on pilings. The front wall of the house is of milled lumber fitted with glass windows. [Schwinke]*

6. *The Nákwakhdakhw chief standing on his great feast dish, which is in the form of the mythical serpent Sisiutl. This dish ended its days on a grave near the village; only a few fragments of it survive. The painting on the screen is said to represent Raven and his human image.* [Curtis]

ment, tried to avoid anything which "betokened civilization" he dictated standards of dress and appearance to his Indian subjects. No doubt this led to distortions of fact—some of them identifiable—but in the main Curtis was careful to satisfy his critical native informants. Curtis' "tampering" with things as they were was probably a factor in the criticism (still occasionally heard) that he drew from ethnologists, some of whom doubted the accuracy of his information as well as his pictures. There was little need to worry. Curtis' Kwakiutl work was solid ethnography, dramatically written and spectacularly illustrated. When many anthropologists and all popular writers on the subject were proclaiming a curious and erroneous version of the Kwakiutl potlatch based on the tales of uncomprehending travelers and missionaries and a misunderstanding of Boas' information (even by Boas himself), Edward Curtis published a straightforward description of a working and workable potlatch which stands comparison with the best modern analyses of the institution. His descriptions of ceremonial activities and everyday technology are among the best in print. Certainly George Hunt, William Myers, and Edmund Schwinke deserve a great deal of the credit. But Edward Curtis takes the honors as the motivating and guiding force.

"In the Days of Vancouver"

The motion picture brewing in Curtis' mind began to take the shape of a dramatic story of love and war. He still saw the story primarily as the glue that would hold together a series of scenes illustrating every possible aspect and activity of traditional Kwakiutl life. He wrote a rather detailed scenario entitled "In the Days of Vancouver," which he subtitled "a documentary picture of the Kwakiutl tribes, the natives of Vancouver Island" (Appendix 2). In 112 scenes, interspersed with "readers" or titles, Curtis developed the story. It is similar to the final film version in many ways. The greatest differences are in the inclusion of the building of a plankhouse and in the arrival of Captain George Vancouver and his tourist-like visit to the Indian village.

In his comments Curtis clearly stated his goal of showing as many facets of native life as possible. Under Scene 51 in Appendix 2, depicting the attack of the vengeful warriors on a group of fishermen, for example, he wrote that "the object is to show the different activities as well as to give a true story of a war expedition." Scene after scene illustrates his plan that this was to be more than an entertaining drama, based on Indian life, but that it was to be educational, that it should illustrate "so far as possible, the activities of their lives," and that it "be an unquestioned document."

Some of the photography may have been done by this time since many scenes describe exactly the action in the film. On the other hand, Curtis may have followed his written descriptions with meticulously careful photography. We have the impression that very little film ended up on the "cutting room floor." Today's custom of shooting many times more film than will be used in the final picture was not the rule in 1914. Some of the final shots do not appear in this version and were certainly made later, as were some which differ in detail from this scenario.

Probably during the early part of the filming, Curtis wrote a detailed version of the story in language that he described as "the declamatory style of the tribal bards" (1915a:vii). Curtis' version of the declamatory style was stilted and flowery. "Once more, I must fast and languish ere peace can fill my heart. Listen! do I hear a song or do my ears deceive me? Or is my brain still in trance? Truly No! for upon the crest swiftly comes a canoe of cedar. Stately sits Naida, the proud chief's daughter, while sturdy maid-slaves with flashing paddle cut the water. Closer now, and passing, is the canoe of the chieftain's daughter. To my ear is borne her song of pride, of love and longing. It is the daughter of the great war chief. . . ." Here the name has been erased and crossed out and the name "Kenada" written above; then Kenada is crossed out and "Waket" is written below. Curtis' uncertainty and his final settlement on the name Waket indicates that this version of the story precedes the final version. This manuscript, including the Vancouver theme, is almost identical to the story, *In the Land of the Head-Hunters*, eventually published as a booklet.

When what is apparently the next document—the "Outline for Scenario"—was written, the story had been pared down and tightened to its final film version. The characters and incidents are identified by village: Motana, the hero, and his father Kenada, live at Watsulis, which is Deer Island in Beaver Harbour, on whose shores the village of Fort Rupert stands; Waket and his daughter Naida, the heroine, live at Paas or Blunden Harbour; the Sorcerer and his warrior brother Yaklus come from Yilis or Alert Bay.

In preparation for the filming, a simple shooting schedule was prepared which consisted of a list of about 170 shots with locations and rough notes indicating major props and numbers of actors involved (see Appendix 3). The outline is evidence for some sophistication in Curtis' concepts of filmmaking in that shots are grouped according to setting rather than by order of their appearance in the story. Each shot is numbered to indicate its place in the final sequence. It is the barest kind of outline and must have been used rather freely.

The outline itself is a succinct statement of the plot, without the flowery embellishments found in the book, *In the Land of the Head-Hunters*. It does identify the locations of some of the scenes in the finished film. For example, the attack on the village of "Yilis" was actually filmed at Blunden Harbour (fig. 7), a village that in 1914 had a much more aboriginal look than the real Yilis.

The problems of turning the grand ideas, the flowery scenarios, and the sketchy shooting script into a motion picture were enormous in Curtis' time and place. Even today the Kwakiutl villages where some of the scenes were shot are remote, isolated from the ordinary traveler by unpredictable seas and impassible mountains. Blunden Harbour, Cur-

tis' setting for the village of the evil Sorcerer and his warrior brother is one of these. Today it is abandoned and merging again with its forest background (fig. 8). On the other hand, Fort Rupert, the home of Curtis' collaborator George Hunt, and the base of operations in making the film, is today just off the road between the burgeoning town of Port Hardy and the Port Hardy airport, one of the busiest in British Columbia. Rows of trailer houses, homes of the many workers newly arrived to man the mines and mills of the booming North Island, press close to the village. Curtis saw a different Fort Rupert. The water was the highway then. The shelving bottom of Beaver Harbour, named for a Hudson's Bay Company steamer that supplied the fort and trading post in the mid-nineteenth century, prevents any deep draught vessel from approaching the shore. Visitors like Edward Curtis had to be lightered in with all their goods and equipment. The village sits above the beach on a high bank. The only reminders today of the row of "big houses" of old are shallow, rectangular depressions in the grassy strip in front of the frame houses, the last vestiges of the slightly excavated floors. A stone fireplace stands alone at the back of the village. It is the last remnant of the Hudson's Bay Company trading post which lured the resident tribes to leave their ancient village sites and establish a new home here in 1849.

The Fort Rupert of Curtis' photographs (fig. 9) was very different from the village of today, but frame houses had begun to spring up among the remaining old-style dwellings, apparently rendering the village unusable as a setting for his drama of "precontact" times. The village does not appear in the film, except as a row of distant reflections across Beaver Harbour in a few of the canoe scenes (fig. 10).

Out in the bay and partially protecting its waters from the north, lies Deer Island. Two rocky points on the side of the island facing Fort Rupert enclose a small gravel beach. This spot was chosen by Curtis as the setting for much of the action in his story. Although the villages represented in the film are all named—Yilis, Paas, Watsulis—and the

7. *Blunden Harbour in the days of Curtis. The village in 1915 already shows some small frame buildings as well as milled lumber and windows on the fronts of traditional houses. Yet this was one of the least modernized of Kwakiutl villages at the time, and the only one to have been used as a set in Curtis' film. [MPM]*

8. *Blunden Harbour village in 1973. The last traditional plank house in Blunden Harbour collapsed in the late 1950s. The village population had been decreasing over the years, and the few remaining residents left the village for new homes at Tsulquate near Port Hardy a few years before this picture was taken.* [Putnam]

9. *Fort Rupert in the days of Curtis. This village was the home of Curtis' collaborator George Hunt and many of the actors in the film. Deer Island, the site of much of the filming, lies in Beaver Harbour, on whose shores Fort Rupert stands. The large totem pole was commissioned by George Hunt's mother, a Tlingit noblewoman, after a family pole with the same figures had been taken from her village of Tongass, Alaska, by a group of Seattle businessmen in the 1890s. [Curtis]*

10. *The houses of Fort Rupert show faintly on the Vancouver Island shore.*
This photograph of the great Kwakiutl canoes was taken from the shore of
Deer Island. [Head-Hunters]

shooting script mentions "Kwaestums" and "Tsatsisnuqumi," only the real village of Blunden Harbour appears in the existing film or photographs filed with the Copyright Office. All the other village scenes were shot on Deer Island.

The Story

As Curtis made clear in his original proposal and in subsequent documents, he intended the film to illustrate every facet of Kwakiutl culture. He kept to that goal and in a measure accomplished it although he was forced by practical considerations to eliminate some of the activities he had originally planned to include. With his actors and props ready Curtis and his crew proceeded to put together a melodrama of vision quest, love, witchcraft, war, ceremony, revenge, capture, rescue, escape, and triumph! At its Seattle preview, the Moore Theater handbill proclaimed: "Every Participant an Indian and Every Incident True to Native Life" (see fig. 1). The program also outlined the complicated story in the most complete and straightforward version to come from Curtis. This was our chief guide in editing and restoring the film and its titles. The synopsis is given in full below:

To gain power from the spirit forces, Motana, the son of a great chief, goes on a vigil journey. Through the fasting and hardships of the vigil he hopes to gain supernatural strength which will make him a chief not less powerful than his father, Kenada.

First upon a mountain's peak he builds a prayer-fire to the Gods. After long dancing about the sacred flames, he drops from exhaustion, and in vision-sleep the face of a maid appears in the coiling smoke, thus breaking the divine law which forbids the thought of women during the fasting.

Now he must pass another stronger ordeal. Leaving his desecrated fire to go to the Island of the Dead, he meets Naida, the maid of his dream, and woos her. She tells him she is promised to the hideous Sorcerer. Motana bids the maid return to her father and say that when this vigil is over he will come with a wealth of presents and beg her hand in marriage. Now he renews his quest of spirit power and tests his courage by spending the night in the fearful "house of skulls." And to prove his prowess he goes in quest of sea-lions and then achieves the greatest feat of all—the capture of a whale.

Then, for his final invocation to the Gods, Motana again builds his sacred fire upon the heights. While he fasts and dances there about his prayer fire the Sorcerer in a dark glade of the forest has gathered about him fellow workers in evil magic and they sing "short time songs" to destroy him. The Sorcerer sends his daughter to find Motana and in some way get a lock of his hair, that they may destroy his life by incantation. This ever-treacherous plotting woman on seeing Motana asleep by his fire becomes infatuated with him and decides to risk even the wrath of her Sorcerer father and win the love of Motana. When she awakens him with caressing words, he bids her begone, as he is not thinking of women, but of the spirits. With angry threats she departs, but in stealth watches the faster until he drops asleep; then creeping up steals his necklace and a lock of hair, and disappears.

Motana returning asks his father to send messengers demanding the hand of Naida. Her father, Waket, replies to the messengers: "My daughter is promised to the fearful Sorcerer. We fear his magic. If your great chief, Kenada, would have my daughter for his son's wife, bring the Sorcerer's head as a marriage gift." With song and shout they start upon the journey and attack the Sorcerer's village. With song triumphant they return with the Sorcerer's head; and in great pomp of primitive pageantry Naida and Motana are married.

Even while the wedding dancers make merry a cloud of tragedy hangs above them, for Yaklus, the fearful war-chief, returning from a fishing expedition, learns of the attack and is preparing to avenge the death of his brother, the Sorcerer.

In his magnificent high-prowed canoes he starts upon his war of vengeance. It is a tribal law that the war party destroy all who are met, whether friend or foe. While on their foray fishing parties and travelers are encountered.

Then they make their night attack upon the village of Motana. Kenada and his tribesmen give way before the infuriated Yaklus, and amid the smoke and flames of the burning village Motana is wounded and Naida is carried away to captivity.

Yaklus returning to his village gives a great dance of victory. The frenzied warriors demand the life of Naida. Yaklus bids her come and dance for them. If she dances well enough to please him he will spare her life. If not, they will throw her to the "hungry wolves." So well does she dance that Yaklus spares her.

In the sleeping hours Naida sends her fellow captive-slave with a token and message to Motana, who has been revived by the surviving medicine men of his village. When he receives the message from his bride-wife Motana calls for volunteers.

By stealth he rescues her. Yaklus in rage starts in pursuit. Motana, hard pressed, dares the waters of the surging gorge of Hyal, through which he passes in safety. Great was his "water magic." Yaklus attempts to follow, but the raging waters of the gorge sweep upon him and he and his grizzly followers become the prey of the evil ones of the sea.

In the Land of the Head-Hunters

Drawing on the wide knowledge of Indian customs he had gained in the course of his work on *The North American Indian*, Curtis wrote two little books. They were clearly meant to be educational as well as entertaining stories. In the Foreword to the first one, *Indian Days of the Long Ago*, Curtis wrote, "This little book was written in the hope that it would give a more intimate view of Indian life in the old days, in the days when to the farwestern tribe the white race was but a rumor and buffalo roamed the plains in countless numbers. A further desire was to call attention to the great divergencies in Indian life, the number of languages, and the striking differences in dress and habits." Rather than assembling a series of stories on each of the many different varieties of American Indian life he wanted to illustrate, Curtis chose to weave his tale around the life of a young boy of the Flathead tribe, living in what is now western Montana. Two old men, "wanderers," one a Clayoquot from Vancouver Island and the other a Huron from the East Coast, come to the Flatheads and it is through their description of travels and adventures that the "great divergencies of Indian life" are made a part of the story.

Indian Days of the Long Ago was published in 1914. Curtis had already worked among the Kwakiutl when he prepared the book, and some of the photographs and drawings are taken from his Kwakiutl experience. The endpaper of the book is a photograph of three Kwakiutl canoes drifting in quiet waters near Fort Rupert, and is captioned "an illustration from a new book by the same author, uniform with 'Indian days of the long ago' . . . entitled 'In the days of Vancouver'." Before "In the Days of Vancouver" was actually published, however, its title had been changed to *In the Land of the Head-Hunters*. The format of the two publications was essentially the same, but *In the Land of the Head-Hunters* was illustrated with thirty full-page photographs. Each of these was a still from the motion picture, which, by the 1915 publication date of the book, had been completed and was being shown in theaters around the country.

In his Foreword to *In the Land of the Head-Hunters*, Curtis said that the book "had its inception in an outline or scenario for a motion picture drama dealing with the hardy Indians inhabiting northern British Columbia." It was these words, read in a junior high school library in 1940, that gave Bill Holm his first inkling of the existence of a Curtis film. He was very curious about that movie, but little did he guess at that time that years later he would count as close friends some of the very people pictured in Curtis' photographs of the Kwakiutl Indians, that he would hear tales of the making of the film from members of the "original cast," and that finally he would have a hand in restoring and bringing that "motion picture drama" back to life.

V. The Preparations for Filming

Transforming Watsulis (river on flat beach), as the Kwakiutl named Deer Island, into the site of a convincing row of big houses was a remarkable feat, and only one of many that Edward Curtis and his Kwakiutl collaborators accomplished in preparation for making the great film.

Bill Holm had examined Curtis' published stills of the scene many times without suspecting that the five gabled housefronts with their towering frontal poles were props—false fronts with only the forest behind them—until he saw a photograph taken in 1915 showing two with their painted canvas fronts gone, exposing spindly frames against the forest (fig. 11). Careful reexamination of the photographs and comments from Kwakiutl who remembered the "village" confirmed the fact that they were stage houses. Two of the false fronts were more sturdily built of planks, and one may have had side walls as well.

Three fully carved totem poles can be seen in the Curtis photographs. One—a tall, rather flat, frontal pole with a large open mouth as an entrance—was said to have been carved by George Hunt himself, probably for the Deer Island set. It now stands in the Museum of Anthropology at the University of British Columbia. Another, much shorter pole stood beside one of the wooden housefronts; it now stands on the British Columbia campus (fig. 12). The other fully carved pole has disappeared (fig. 13). Whether it exists today is not known, but it was a magnificent one, inspired by the great Raven pole of Wakyas, the first fully carved tall pole at Alert Bay (fig. 14), which now stands extensively restored in Vancouver's Stanley Park. The Raven frontal pole at Deer Island was probably made for the film (it doesn't appear in any photographs of Fort Rupert or other villages), and it seems to be newly carved and painted in Curtis' pictures. A later photograph shows the housefront collapsing and the great articulated Raven's beak gone (Barbeau 1950:fig. 409). The pole probably rotted and fell onto the beach, where its carved and painted fragments were smoothed and scattered by the changing waters.

Only a few people today remember these carvings at all. Perhaps fifteen or twenty years ago more specific information might have been gathered from carvers who were actively carving at the time the Deer Island poles were made. Unfortunately, twenty years ago Holm had no idea that he would eventually be involved in the restoration of Curtis' historic film and much of the information he gathered was casual and without focus. Mungo Martin suggested that George Hunt carved the tall, flat pole and that Charlie James made the Thunderbird and Grizzly houseposts, but Holm has no notes which shed any light on when or for what purpose they were carved.

A few tantalizing clues are left to us in Curtis' shooting script. He mentioned the "artificial houses" of Waket, Motana, and Yaklus, and in the schedule of scenes to be shot at Blunden Harbour is the parenthetical note to "take over 2 new totems" (Appendix 3). In any case an enormous amount of work went into the preparation of the sets for the film. There are five "poles" visible in the pictures of the Watsulis village. Of these, one is painted on flat planks applied to the front wall (fig. 12). One appears to have been a plain pole on which some figures have been constructed by adding simple wings, beaks, and snouts. The "George Hunt" pole is sculptured in low relief on a half-cylindrical log section, with a long beak morticed on. In its present form the beak, which was missing when the pole was collected, has been replaced with a short curved Thunderbird's beak. The short, free-

11. *One year after the making of the film, the artificial village on Deer Island presented this appearance. Some of the house fronts were made of canvas on light pole frames that can be seen in this picture, after the cloth had been removed by man or weather. [MPM]*

12. *One of the more substantial false house fronts on Deer Island. The house frontal pole has been painted on a flat board. It probably represents a whale with long pectoral fins spread across the house front, and tail flukes rising above the roof line. The short fully carved entrance pole, representing Thunderbird and Whale over some unknown creature, is now in the collection of the University of British Columbia Museum of Anthropology. [Schwinke]*

standing entrance pole is carved in traditional Kwakiutl style with the figures of Thunderbird and Whale, and with a humanoid face whose open mouth forms the entrance (fig. 12). The imposing entrance pole of Kenada's house is fully sculptured with figures of a man, Thunderbird, Hokhokw, Grizzly, and the great Raven, whose wings, tail and legs spread in elaborate painting over the facade of the house (fig. 13). It was more expertly carved than its predecessor in Alert Bay (fig. 14) and lacks only Wolf and Killerwhale to be a virtual copy.

The interior scenes with the towering Thunderbird and Grizzly houseposts are completely convincing. They seem to be photographed in a real house, with perhaps some of the roof planks removed to allow light for photography. But no shadows fall on the poles or the floor from the giant beams which would have rested on these monumental houseposts if this were a real house. In one dance picture published in *In the Land of the Head-Hunters* (p. 79), the end of a crossbeam can be seen resting on the head of one of the Thunderbird figures and its shadow falls on the wall in back of the poles (fig. 15). Yet the area of the picture that should show the roof structure is devoid of eave beams, rafters, or purlins, and only a vague dark area with splotches that suggest branches and tree trunks of a forest can be seen. The whole floor and the assembled actors are in bright, uninterrupted sunlight. There is no roof, not even a frame of one, on this "house." When the Schwinke photographs came to light the mystery of the house was essentially solved. It was indeed a stage set, an imitation house consisting of a back wall, two carved houseposts and their connecting crossbeam, and short side walls. It could not have been a partially dismantled house since (strangely, considering Edward Curtis' passion for authenticity) the framing for the wall is invisible, being on the outside, rather than on the inside as

13. *The most spectacular of the carvings on Deer Island was the great Raven entrance pole. It was apparently carved for the film, stood only on this spot, and weathered away here. At least no part of it has been located in any present-day collection. [Schwinke]*

in a typical Kwakiutl house. Schwinke's photographs show the temporary quality of the side wall panels very clearly. In fact, in his earliest pictures of the house the left panel has not yet been erected (fig. 16).

Where this false house was built, and the age of the carved posts, are more difficult questions, but even answers to them might lie in the Schwinke photographs, taken together with Curtis' shooting script and the second recent and very remarkable discovery: George Hunt's ledger record of part of his work for Edward Curtis. In the mid-1970s this extremely important document was given in a Kwakiutl potlatch to Don Lelooska, who very generously made it available for study. It is in the form of a bound ledger containing entries of four kinds, all in George Hunt's hand. Most typical for Kwakiutl ledgers are the records of payments and debts related to Hunt's potlatching activities. In addition the ledger contains records of manuscripts sent to Franz Boas and payments for them received by Hunt from Columbia University and the Bureau of American Ethnology (typically 33⅓ cents per page). But the real surprise in the Hunt ledger is a record, consisting of eight pages, of work related to the making of Edward Curtis' film. This record, covering the preparations from October 1912 to October 1913, and a single page listing days worked by sixteen people in April and May of 1914, underscore the major role which George Hunt played in filming *In the Land of the Head-Hunters*.

On page 17 of the ledger, at the end of a list of masks "bought for Mr. E. S. Curtis" in March of 1913, are listed two totem poles purchased on 16 June 1913, for $90.50 and $75.00 (Appendix 6). These could have been two of the poles for the Deer Island village, but there is the probability that they are the houseposts for the interior setting.

14. *The prototype of the Deer Island Raven entrance pole was the famous pole belonging to Chief Wakyas of Alert Bay, seen here in Edward Curtis' photograph. As on the Deer Island pole, the Raven's beak could be opened to serve as the ceremonial entrance to the house. The restored pole stands in Stanley Park, Vancouver, British Columbia. [Curtis]*

15. *An elaborate set consisting of a pair of houseposts and connecting beam, an end wall, and part of a side wall was constructed to simulate a house interior. Curtis carefully avoided photographing beyond the edges of the false walls to preserve the illusion of an actual house. Even so, some shots do show some of the forest where the walls or roof should be, as in this dance scene. [Head-Hunters]*

16. *Edmund Schwinke's snapshot of two masked dancers shows the lack of a side wall on the artificial house. The motion picture camera on its tripod stands at the side. Leaning against blankets piled around a carved figure is a great copper. It and the blankets were used in the scene of the marriage of Motana and Naida. Unfortunately much of this part of the film is missing. The interior houseposts for the set were probably made for this purpose. The fierce Grizzlies and Thunderbirds are similar to figures on a slightly older pair of houseposts which still stand in Alert Bay. [Schwinke]*

17. *Edward Curtis at Blunden Harbour, surrounded by members of the cast. This lighthearted group portrait of the filmmaker and actors says a great deal about the atmosphere of the project. The surviving participants recall the reconstruction of the ways of their old people as exciting and enjoyable. Little girls are casually holding the gruesome "trophy heads." [Schwinke]*

There are no totems at all evident in Curtis' exterior shots of Blunden Harbour, and Schwinke's photograph (fig. 17), taken in front of a Blunden Harbour house, shows Curtis surrounded by costumed actors, including women and children, as they appeared in the interior scenes. It seems likely now that the interior set was built at Blunden Harbour using newly carved poles brought over from Fort Rupert. The price of $165.50 paid for the two poles seems consistent with values of the time, given that Curtis paid $15.00 for the most expensive mask he bought, an elaborate representation of a whale.

Curtis used this same interior for every house in which carved posts show. With bare plank walls and winged Thunderbirds, it is the house of Waket, the father of the heroine Naida (fig. 18). Remove the birds' wings, raise the many-mouthed cannibal pole between the houseposts, hang animal skins on the walls, erect the Mawihl or secret room for the Hamatsa, and cover the grizzlies' bodies with carvings of the Dzoonokwa, the man-eating giantess, and the house of the merciless war chief Yaklus emerges (fig. 19). The Dzoonokwa carvings that disguise the poles do not appear to have had any other function, and seem to have been made solely for this purpose. If so, they are another illustration of the lengths to which Curtis went in achieving the effects he wanted.

The striking pole between the houseposts, with its superimposed open-mouthed faces, was also newly carved. Its name is *humspek* (cannibal pole), and it belongs to a spectacular variant of the *hamatsa*, or "man-eater dance." Although Curtis briefly described its use in a footnote in the Kwakiutl volume of *The North American Indian* (1915b:175), it appears in the film only as an impressive decoration. Franz Boas published, in both English and Kwakwala, a detailed account from the Awaitlula tribe of the origin of the carved *humspek* (Boas 1910:415–42). While Boas' graphic description, which is illustrated with an Indian drawing, mentions four open mouths, Curtis describes "five huge faces with enormous mouths." None of his published photographs, or the motion picture film, show the top of the *humspek*, and only four faces are visible. Schwinke's pictures show the entire pole with its traditional *four* faces.

The Hamatsa initiate, dramatizing his ancestor's encounter with the cannibal spirit Bakhbakwalanookswey, climbs the pole and descends head first, in one mouth and out the next. The last Awaitlula owner of the dance to use the *humspek* in this way was a young man at the time of the filming, and the pole was probably made for him. If it exists today its location is not known. His songs have been used in recent winter dances by his heirs, with the *humspek* represented by a quickly made painting on corrugated cardboard. The Hamatsa, of course, could not slither through the mouths of the cardboard *humspek*, but he made the gestures appropriate to the words when the pole was mentioned in his songs. A similar and perhaps more traditional *humspek* stands in the reconstructed Kwakiutl house, Wa'waditla, at the Provincial Museum in Victoria, British Columbia. In the spring of 1977 a copy of this *humspek* was carved by Richard Hunt, a great grandson of George Hunt, and was used by the present owner of the dance in a Winter Ceremonial at Alert Bay. The carver of one *humspek*, perhaps the one in Victoria, was said to have lost his senses when, during the carving, the various mouths came alive as in the origin myth; he died shortly thereafter.

Some of the masks and other carved objects were probably made especially for use in the film, although these are harder to document than large poles. George Hunt lists twenty-one masks (and their prices) purchased for Curtis in 1913 (Appendix 6). At least some of these were older pieces but many must have been newly made for the occasion. There is clear evidence for only one new one: a payment of five dollars on 23 August 1913, to "Johnny" for making a Hokhokw mask. One of Hunt's lists is labeled "Tools Bought to work the mask with for Mr. E. S. Curtis 1913." It lists files, sand paper, saws, a "Bended carvers Knife," paint, dye for cedar bark, and fifty-six skins of various animals and birds including eleven eagles, five swans, three grizzly bears, and eight mountain goats.

A number of the masks that appear in the motion picture or in other Curtis Kwakiutl photographs have made their way into collections. The awesome Bukwus mask, which appears in Curtis' Kwakiutl volume

18. *The basic stage set for the house interior is shown in this Schwinke photograph. The complete lack of roof beams and framing, made necessary by the need for full sky light, is clearly seen. A settee, or long seat, has been placed on the platform between the house posts. In this form the set represents the house of Waket, the father of the heroine Naida. [Schwinke]*

19. *The house of Yaklus, the merciless war chief, is the same set with some simple additions. The* humspek, *or cannibal pole, is the most spectacular of them. The house posts have been altered by removal of the Thunderbird wings and the addition of the heads and torsos of the Dzoonokwa, a mythical giant. The rectangular painted panel at the left is the* mawihl, *a screen which forms a cubicle for the Hamatsa, or cannibal dancer, initiate. It is surrounded by garlands of hemlock boughs, an emblem of the Winter Ceremonial. [Schwinke]*

(1915:158, 166), is in the Samuel Barrett collection in the Milwaukee Public Museum (Mochon 1966:figs. 68–69). It was collected in 1915, not long after Curtis photographed it, and shows signs of age and wear. Several other masks photographed by Curtis were also collected by Barrett at that time and are now in Milwaukee. None of them appears to be new. An old Raven mask seen in the film and in volume 10 (p. 234) is now in a Seattle collection. It was likely made before 1900. The whale-rib clubs carried by the warriors and the sorcerers in the film were apparently newly made. They were collected by Edward Curtis and are now in the Burke Museum collections.

Many ceremonial and utilitarian objects of native manufacture were in use, or at least still available, in Curtis' time. The great animal-form feast dishes and ladles that figure so prominently in wedding scenes must have been old family pieces. The spruce-root basketry hats were prized in 1914 as they are today. Many of them were made by Haida or Tlingit weavers and traded or sold to the Vancouver Island people, who painted them in their own stylistic tradition. Those in the film were probably not new.

A few pieces of twined yellow cedar-bark clothing and some robes, capes, and skirts had survived until the making of the film and were used by the actors. Since Curtis' plan was to illustrate the pre-trade period culture, however, he needed enough aboriginal-style clothing to outfit all his actors. He went to fur (and imitation fur) robes and kilts and skin tunics, recalling hide armor, for the warriors in his story. For the rest of the needed clothing he commissioned Indian women to shred and twine cedar bark for robes. Because of the scarcity of cedar bark, either prepared or stored, or perhaps because of the practical seasonal limitation on gathering cedar bark or the lack of time, Curtis was forced to furnish raffia to the native craftswomen in order to complete enough robes for the cast. Mrs. George Hunt was often mentioned by Kwakiutl who recalled the making of the film as one who worked on these garments. Hunt's ledger presents a graphic picture of the magnitude of this effort. "Mrs. David" (Sarah Smith Hunt, his daughter-in-law) was paid one dollar for "sewing 8 grass (rafia) blankets" and Mrs. George Hunt was listed as making thirty blankets, ten capes, eight grass aprons, three neck rings, and beating cedar bark for a total payment of seventy-seven dollars. Some of these items, especially those of raffia, were very roughly made, with the rows of twining which held the "bark" warp together spaced several inches apart, in contrast to older yellow cedar-bark pieces in which the fine rows of twining are often less than half an inch apart. Raffia kilts were also fabricated to complete some of the dance costumes. All these are easily recognized in the Curtis photographs by their flimsy, stringy quality in contrast to the fullness of the traditional material.

Ceremonial cedar-bark regalia was also made to supplement the traditional headrings and neckrings kept for the winter dances. What appear to be the largest such rings ever seen were made for Curtis' pictures. Again Mrs. Hunt is named by Kwakiutl informants as the maker. Although her rings do not appear in the surviving film, they are pictured in the Kwakiutl volume worn by a Hamatsa dressed for his last dance (Curtis 1915:182). They are now in the Burke Museum collection.

Of all the artifacts used in the film, by far the most spectacular are the canoes. Without any doubt the canoe scenes are the most popular in the film, especially those of a great canoe racing by with the masked Thunderbird dancer "flying" in the bow, and the approach of the wedding party with Thunderbird, Wasp, and Grizzly Bear dancing to the beat of paddles on the gunwales. The tiny canoes used by Naida and Motana are beautifully buoyant and graceful. There is an ease born of familiarity and long experience with which the hero handles his little one-man craft. Warriors work their great canoe around a rocky point or leap aboard in the surf and race across a choppy bay with casual skill. But we are witnessing here the very end of the canoe life on the Northwest Coast. Curtis used about six canoes in the film, which were probably all he could easily assemble at Fort Rupert. Pictures taken in the Kwakiutl villages only about a decade before show twenty or more canoes drawn up on each village beach. By the passing of another decade

20. *The largest of the three large canoes used by Curtis was over fifty feet
long. In 1914 only a very few such canoes remained. This one was painted
with the figure of the mythical serpent Sisiutl. In order to increase the apparent
size of his fleet, Curtis had this canoe disguised by painting over the Sisiutl.
[Schwinke]*

even the canoes Curtis photographed were rotting away or gone, and only an isolated few narrow river canoes survive in the Kwakiutl country today.

The largest of the three large canoes in Curtis' film was around fifty feet long, with a beam of perhaps seven feet (fig. 20). This is a large canoe by any standard, but much larger canoes were known on the coast. Since he apparently had only these three large canoes available, Curtis resorted to another trick of disguise to increase the apparent number. The war canoe of Yaklus is none other than the great Sisiutl canoe of his rival and victim, Kenada, with the design of the horned serpent Sisiutl obliterated with black paint. By identifying the same canoes, in disguise, with different people and places, Curtis gave the impression of a plethora of canoes (true for old Kwakiutl culture). At least one of these canoes was purchased by Curtis for use in the film, and he also paid for materials and work in patching them. Hunt's records list paddles and paint for paddles that he bought for Curtis.

The Actors

George Hunt, who had been of so much help to Edward Curtis in his Kwakiutl research, was the one perfectly suited to assist him in making the film. Much of Curtis' text comes directly from Hunt, and much of that obtained from other sources was filtered through him as interpreter. George Hunt was well qualified for the job. Although not Kwakiutl by birth, he was born and raised at Fort Rupert, and long before he became Edward Curtis' associate, in his sixties, he had reached high status among the Kwakiutl tribes. His influence is recognizable throughout Curtis' writing and no less in the film, *In the Land of the Head-Hunters*. With the newly discovered Schwinke photographs and Hunt's ledger, the importance of George Hunt to Curtis' work is made vastly more apparent. The enormously complex job of organizing the work to be done on the masks, canoes, imitation houses, and costumes of the actors fell on his shoulders. He hired those who worked on these props and those who played the parts. It is no exaggeration to say that Hunt not only furnished Edward Curtis with much of the factual information which formed the basis of the movie, but also acted as intermediary and interpreter while Curtis was present and as Curtis' representative while he was not. Just as Hunt was essential to Boas' Kwakiutl work, so was he to Curtis' work. Many of the actors were Hunt's children and grandchildren, or were otherwise closely related to him. There was good reason for this, mainly because these people were available and amenable to directions from Hunt. They were also handsome and talented, which suited Curtis just fine. Hunt's active part in the direction of the filming is graphically recorded in Schwinke's photographs of Curtis behind his camera and George Hunt, megaphone in hand, directing the actors (figs. 21 and 22).

In selecting his actors Curtis made some choices which are hard to explain. For some reason he used three different women to play the part of the heroine Naida. It may be that they were available at different times, or perhaps he actually had trouble keeping one of them on the job in the face of opposition by her relatives, as he describes in a dramatic article, "Filming the Head-Hunters," published in *Strand Magazine* in 1915 (Appendix 4). Although there is much good information on Kwakiutl customs in the article, this description of making the film is exaggerated and riddled with inaccuracies. On the whole it is an interesting account, which probably says more about 1915 film promotion than about the facts of "filming the head-hunters." For whatever reason, there are three Naidas, one of whom seems to have played yet another major role! To add to the confusion, two of the male leads were played by the same man, if identifications by present-day Kwakiutl viewers are accurate. As mentioned before, disguised posts and repainted canoes enabled Curtis to double the usefulness of his props, and to top it all off, the same beach was used over and over again as the place of embarkation and landing of many a canoe voyage, no matter where it was supposed to be going or from where it was coming. Curtis was completely consistent in his inconsistency.

21. *The importance of George Hunt to the success of the project is illustrated
by this picture of Hunt and Curtis during the filming. Megaphone in hand,
George Hunt directs the action in this scene of Naida's dance for her captors.
This incident was included in the story* In the Land of the Head-Hunters,
but has been lost to the film as it exists today. [Schwinke]

The heroine, Naida, first appears in a title shot played by Margaret Wilson Frank. Mrs. Frank was one of those who viewed the film several times during the early stages of planning its restoration. Her parents were Charlie Wilson, a chief at Fort Rupert, and Emily Hunt Wilson, a daughter of George Hunt.

The second Naida to appear is Sarah Smith Martin. Mrs. Martin at the time of the filming was the wife of David Hunt, George Hunt's eldest son. She was the daughter of a chief at Turnour Island and was renowned as a dancer. Later she married Mungo Martin and was fondly and respectfully known as Abayah (roughly the equivalent of "Mom") until her death in 1963.

The third Naida apparently appears only once near the end of the film in the scene of the escape from Yaklus' house. She has been identified as Mrs. George Walkus, Gwikilaokwa, of Smith Inlet, and is said to have died not long after the filming. Mrs. Walkus also was identified in the film as the daughter of the Sorcerer, sent to steal the hero Motana's hair and neckring for use in witchcraft.

The name "Naida" was apparently coined by Curtis. No Kwakiutl questioned on the matter knew any traditional name resembling it. On the other hand the name "Motana" was regularly recognized as an Awíkenokhw Hamatsa named Moo'dana, which Curtis translates "Four Man eater." The part of Motana was played by Stanley Hunt, George Hunt's youngest son (fig. 23).

Motana's father, Kenada, was played by Paddy Maleed, a Nákwakhdakhw of Blunden Harbour (fig. 24). He was also known to informants as Kimgidi. Most of the principals were from Fort Rupert and Blunden Harbour.

The man who, according to every person old enough to identify the characters, played both the part of Waket, Naida's father, and that of Yaklus, the war-chief brother of the Sorcerer, was known as Bulóotsa (fig. 25). This is said to be a Kwakiutlization of the English name Brotchie. Bulóotsa was also Nákwakhdakhw of Blunden Harbour. Neither the name Waket nor Yaklus was recognized. A character in an Awaitlula myth published by Curtis in volume 10, page 289, is named Wáhèt. This may well be the source. An unpublished note in the Curtis manuscript material in the Los Angeles County Museum of Natural History translates the name "Rock Broken." One man thought Waket might have come from the Tsimshian name Weégyet, and the name Yaklus has a Kwakiutl ring. The consensus was that Curtis coined both names. There is a good reason for him to have done so, since to use actual names could invite criticism from the living owners of those hereditary titles. William Halliday, the agent of the Kwawkewlth Agency for many years, and a great foe of the potlatch, was severely criticized for using real names in his book *Potlatch and Totem*.

The fact that one man played two major parts (and perhaps a third minor role) and that three women played the female lead was the source of a great deal of confusion on the part of older Kwakiutl who viewed the unedited film. Bulóotsa was Bulóotsa, and each of the three women had her own identity, so Curtis' characters could not easily be defined. The same viewers always saw the beach at Deer Island when Curtis intended them to see Yilis, Paas, and Watsulis. Audiences unfamiliar with the actors or with the geography of the Kwakiutl country have no such trouble.

The part of the evil Sorcerer was played by Kwa'kwaano, a noted singer and composer, half Nákwakhdakhw and half Kwagyoohl. He was also known as Haéytlulas and Long Harry. The Sorcerer is seen in the film with long, matted hair. The rest of the male characters also have long hair, although Kwakiutl men had worn their hair short for more than a generation by this time. Curtis furnished them wigs, as is certainly obvious in some cases. He also required the men to shave off their mustaches, either under the mistaken impression that mustaches were not aboriginal with the Kwakiutl or, more likely, because he believed that white audiences wouldn't accept them as "authentic." He paid the men who shaved; the amount is said to have been fifty cents apiece. Kwa'kwaano was one of the few who remained unshaven.

All the actors were paid, the amount usually mentioned was fifty

22. *The extras on the sidelines enjoy the action of the principles in this scene from the wedding festivities. Curtis operates the motion picture camera, George Hunt waits with his megaphone, the plate camera and an extra tripod stand ready, while Edmund Schwinke photographs the whole scene with his folding Kodak. [Schwinke]*

cents per day. This is always described as "good pay for those days." The principal actors received more.

The other parts were taken by the men, women, and children of Fort Rupert and Blunden Harbour (fig. 26). Some of them are known, or in some way stand out. Tsukwani, Mrs. George Hunt, is seen frequently in the film dancing, digging clams, captured by a war party, and so on. Bob Wilson appears in the film and also helped in transporting the actors to Deer Island. He and his sisters, Helen Knox and Margaret Frank (both in the film), have been of great help in reconstructing the happenings of sixty years ago. These three grandchildren of George Hunt are among the many of his descendants and relatives who participated in making the film. The dominance of George Hunt in Kwakiutl studies is striking. He was an interpreter, informant, collaborator, and assistant to Adrian Jacobsen, Franz Boas, Edward Curtis, and Samuel Barrett, all people who made major contributions to the assembled body of knowledge on the Kwakiutl. Our understanding of Kwakiutl culture is largely due to his efforts and perhaps colored by his personal bias. His descendants are still today at the forefront of traditional activities among the northern Vancouver Island people.

23. *The hero Motana, played by Stanley Hunt, George Hunt's youngest son. The carved wolf figure is a traditional Kwakiutl feast dish, a prestigious object of family ownership, just as is the Grizzly Bear and Thunderbird housepost beside Motana. The box-like container on the back of the wolf dish is a feast bowl from one of the northern coastal tribes, probably the Bella Bella. [Schwinke]*

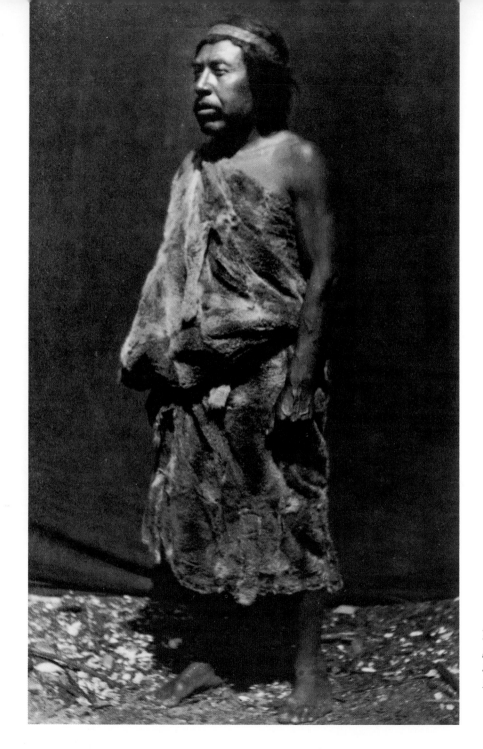

24. *Paddy Maleed in the role of Kenada, father of the hero. Maleed was of a generation which knew some of the old ways of life through personal experience and whose grandparents lived in the time Curtis intended to represent in his film. [Schwinke]*

25. *Yaklus, the fierce war chief, played by Bulóotsa, brandishes trophy heads and a double-bladed dagger. This knife was collected by Curtis and is now in the Burke Museum. It may have been made for the film. Northwest Coast warriors once took heads as war trophies, and Curtis made the most of the custom in his film. A photograph much like this one, taken at the same time, was published in the 1915* Strand *article where the warrior was described as only recently tamed! In fact the last Kwakiutl wars were long over before Bulóotsa was born. [Schwinke]*

26. *The most charming of Schwinke's photographs is this one of three little girls in costume, passing the time between takes. One works on a miniature basket, while Curtis at his camera goes on with his filming in the background. Mrs. Helen Knox identified herself as one of the girls. [Schwinke]*

VI. In the Land of the War Canoes

The film, in its restored version, opens with a spectacular scene of great canoes, racing past the viewer with driving paddles, a feathered and masked Thunderbird dancer in the bow. This scene exemplifies the drama of ancient Kwakiutl life and the preeminence of the canoe in Kwakiutl culture. Curtis' original title *In the Land of the Head-Hunters* was revised for the restored, sound version of the film to *In the Land of the War Canoes*. The original title put undue emphasis on what was actually a minor if visible and spectacular aspect of Kwakiutl life. No doubt Curtis saw a box office advantage in the reference to headhunting, but the implication is that the custom was more important than it actually was. There was no headhunting cult nor elaborate ritualization of head taking among the Kwakiutl. Heads were war trophies, not central features of ceremonialism. On the other hand the canoe was not only central to Kwakiutl traditional life, but is directly or indirectly part of every scene in the film.

Originally the principal characters were identified with titled portraits at the opening of the film. Only one of these portraits—a profile of Naida, the proud princess—survived the ravages of time and fire which damaged the only print known. Her headdress of plaited cedar bark, abalone shell, dentalium shell, and ermine is in the Burke Museum collections. It is somewhat unusual in form and today its use is considered an inherited privilege. Naida is wearing a nose ring of abalone shell. Margaret Frank, the actress in this shot of Naida, remembered the nose ring because it tickled when she wore it. In reconstructing the film, the portraits of the other principals were taken from Curtis' published still photographs.

The Action

THROUGH FASTING AND HARDSHIPS, MOTANA, THE SON OF A GREAT CHIEF, KENADA, SEEKS SUPERNATURAL POWER. IN HIS VISION-SLEEP THE FACE OF A MAIDEN APPEARS TO HIM. IT IS NAIDA, THE DAUGHTER OF CHIEF WAKET.

Motana has gone to a secluded spot to seek supernatural power. By fasting and ritual purification he hopes to make himself acceptable to the spirits which might come to him. Motana dances around the fire in somewhat the manner of a Hamatsa, or cannibal dancer. Whether this was characteristic of power seekers, or just an acceptable action for the film could not be ascertained. The power quest has been so long gone from Kwakiutl experience that none of the people who viewed the scene could explain it.

When Motana finally lies down beside his fire he dreams, but not of supernatural power. His vision is of the beautiful Naida. In this scene Curtis made use of one of photography's unique attributes in producing the image of Naida's face in the smoke of Motana's fire.

MOTANA LEAVES HIS VIGIL AND WOOS NAIDA. SHE IS PROMISED TO AN OLD SORCERER WHO WATCHES THE LOVERS FROM HIDING. MOTANA VOWS TO WIN NAIDA'S HAND.

Motana leaves his vigil and goes to meet Naida, who arrives in her small canoe. The sudden jump in the position of the canoe, from far to near, is the result of frames lost through damage to the original film. Motana hands something to her. This was interpreted as being a token of his love. He watches her disappear in the reflection of the sunset. Motana embarks in his own small canoe and overtakes her. Their visit is watched by the evil Sorcerer to whom Naida has been promised by her father Waket. Naida, of course, has no interest in this and she accepts Motana's plan to make his own proposal to her father. The Sorcerer is angered by this turn of events and plans to destroy Motana.

HE RESUMES HIS SPIRIT QUEST AT THE ISLAND OF THE DEAD. THEN TESTING HIS COURAGE AND SKILLS HE HARPOONS THE SEALION AND WHALE.

Motana enters what seems to be a grave house and dances with a neckring of skulls. Finally he lays his head on a pillow of skulls in his quest for supernatural contact.

Men sometimes prepared for acquiring power by handling corpses, washing with the clothing of the dead or sleeping on skulls. Curtis implies that this scene takes place in a grave house, but it appears to be a reproduction of a shrine such as the "purifying house" of the Nootka whaler Ts!akhwasap, as described and pictured in Boas' *Religion of the Kwakiutl Indians* (1930:257–69). There are still grave houses and a few tree burials around the Kwakiutl villages. Many of the grave houses are in a state of deterioration and corpses and skeletons are occasionally exposed. In Curtis' time it would have been fairly easy to gather the props for this scene. The Kwakiutl do not like to have anything to do with human remains even now, which probably explains some of the feelings of awe accorded power seekers who handled them. A few years ago Holm found a fragment of a jaw from a burial on the site of a modern house which had burned down. The owner of the house was surprised that it had been built over a grave and concluded that the troubles he had had with his house were the result of this indiscretion.

Recently a group of photographs from the Curtis estate were exhibited and reproduced in a small catalogue (Rice 1976). Among them were pictures of a man, acting as a Hamatsa, handling and smoking a mummified body in supposed preparation for a mummy feast. In the same group of photographs a woman dressed as Kominoka (a female associate of the Cannibal Spirit) carries the dessicated leg of a corpse and contemplates a skull attached to her cedar bark neckring. The pictures were not published in any of Curtis' works and may have been made in secret. Who are these old Kwakiutl who were willing to pose? Mrs. George Hunt is the Kominoka, and George Hunt himself with wig and blackened face is the Hamatsa.

The sealion hunt is another piece of Curtis' pastiche of Kwakiutl customs. Hunting sealions was a normal activity for young men, not a test of courage or manhood. The approach of the sealion hunters in their graceful canoe is one of the most natural and believable scenes in the film (fig. 27).

The sealions were photographed at Pearl Rock near Cape Calvert, north of Vancouver Island. The scene has been variously identified as being near Cape Scott at the northwestern extremity of Vancouver Island, and as being off Long Beach in the Ucluelet-Tofino area on Vancouver Island's west coast. Thomas Hunt, nephew of Stanley Hunt, the Motana of the film, and a fisherman intimately familiar with the islands and waters of the area, made the Pearl Island identification. His father David Hunt, Stanley's older brother, accompanied Edward Curtis, his cameraman, and Stanley to the rock on Harry T. Cadwallader's boat.

The northern, or Steller, sealions congregate in great numbers on the rocky islets of the coast. Curtis' shot of the avalanche of sealions cascading from Pearl Rock never fails to draw gasps of amazement from the audience. Just when it appears that all the sealions have dived into the sea, there is a fresh surge of the animals plunging off the rock. Bull Steller sealions are big and aggressive, and in their own element on the bare rocks of the Pacific.

Landing on such a rock is difficult under the best conditions, but the little party was put ashore with camera and equipment and the boat returned to Safety Cove where it was anchored. Schwinke's photo of Cadwallader's boat (fig. 28) may have been taken from the rock since it follows in number sequence a picture of the barren island. The night

27. *Sea mammals were hunted from small canoes carrying two men, one the harpooner and the other the steersman. Hunting canoes were sleek and narrow and were carefully maintained to protect their polished hulls. In this picture Motana and his steersman paddle toward the sealion rocks. The double-pronged harpoon is carried in a notch in the bow of the canoe, called "the resting place of the harpoon."* [LC]

28. *Harry Cadwallader's boat* Hesperus *was used by Curtis to transport his crew and equipment among the islands and inlets of the northern Vancouver Island area. This picture was taken on the trip to the desolate Pearl Rocks, thirty some miles north of Vancouver Island, where the sealion hunting scene was shot. Harry Cadwallader was an American who had moved to Vancouver Island and married one of George Hunt's daughters. He kept a store at Fort Rupert, the last vestige of the Hudson's Bay Company trading post from which the village gets its name. His little boat, formerly schooner rigged (like Longfellow's* Hesperus*) carried goods and supplies to outlying villages and logging camps. [Schwinke]*

on Pearl Rock was apparently uneventful, although a harrowing story of near tragedy has been told of that night's stay. Curtis himself may have exaggerated the adventure of photographing life on the Northwest Coast. The story goes that after the little party had landed and their only means of escape, Cadwallader's boat, had left, they discovered that the island would be swept by waves at high tide. By lashing themselves and their equipment to the rocks they managed to survive the ordeal, and went on the next morning to complete the photography. The story is full of loopholes, but the main clues to its fictional character are that no Kwakiutl informant remembers the tide incident although the slightest misadventures in any endeavor are typically recalled with relish. Furthermore, David Hunt, an experienced seaman who had fished, hunted, and trapped over the area all his life (he was then in his late thirties), would never have put Curtis' party, which included Hunt's own younger brother, ashore on an island that would be under water before Cadwallader returned. The story by implication makes Cadwallader and David Hunt negligent, if not stupid, and suggests an ignorance of tidal action on the part of people whose lives were regulated by the tides.

In the film, Motana approaches the unseen sealions with his long harpoon ready and the harpoon line coiled. We have no evidence that Curtis photographed the actual strike, or even the throwing of the harpoon, but he may have since some footage is missing at this point judging from the prints of individual frames in the Copyright Office.

In the whale hunt sequence Curtis again used his film as a vehicle for illustrating customs on the Northwest Coast, in this case from the Nootkan tribes. The Kwakiutl historically were not whale hunters, although there is a tradition of whale hunting among the people of the Quatsino Sound area. It seems clear, however, that it was Curtis' intent to show a spectacular activity which was part of the general Northwest Coast, even Vancouver Island, culture. Interestingly, the 'whaling' scenes were shot far to the north, at Naden Harbour in the Queen Charlotte Islands. Curtis took Stanley Hunt there, according to the recollections of many people, including Stanley's sister, Mary Hunt Johnson. At a whaling station there the great whale that Motana "killed" was borrowed for the occasion (fig. 29). Curtis' statement (if in fact it is his and not the interviewer's) in the *Strand* article (Appendix 4) is pure embellishment: "And a mighty tough job it was" he was quoted, "for the whale put up a hard fight. Killing a ninety-foot amphibian [sic] and towing him back to shore is no easy morning's diversion, I can assure you." All the canoes and their crews were Haida, who like the Kwakiutl were not whalers.

The scenes of Motana in his bearskin robe, his men towing the whale, and the awarding of the portions are reminiscent of Curtis' Nootka photographs in volume 11 of *The North American Indian*.

THE JEALOUS SORCERER PLOTS TO DESTROY MOTANA AND SENDS HIS DAUGHTER TO FIND HIM AND GET A LOCK OF HIS HAIR.

Witchcraft was a feature of Northwest Coast life that gave Curtis a particularly dramatic theme. It has not been long gone from Kwakiutl life and the response from some who viewed the film was grave. This was especially true of people from the isolated and conservative villages. Almost everyone immediately recognized what was happening.

The older Sorcerer, having seen Naida and Motana together and determining to destroy Motana by witchcraft, gathers his assistants in a secret spot deep in the woods. The practitioner of sorcery, or *eyka*, was likely to be known and could be hired to cast his spell on an unsuspecting victim, with the aid of objects or materials that had been in contact with the body of the proposed victim or his fingernail clippings or strands of hair. The spell over these objects was intended to affect their owner and result in his death. It is said that people were very careful to destroy hair combings or nail clippings to prevent their falling into witches' hands. Even spitting on the ground could be dangerous as the saliva might be obtained by a sorcerer. The work was always carried out in secret, since anyone discovered in the act or proven to have practiced *eyka* would be killed. Sorcerers often went about their work armed with

29. *The great whale "killed" by Motana was actually one borrowed from a commercial whaling station in Naden Harbour, Queen Charlotte Islands. Curtis hired Haida canoes and crews for this sequence, bringing only Stanley Hunt from Vancouver Island to play Motana. [Head-Hunters]*

their whalebone warclubs, as do those in Curtis' film. George Hunt gave both Boas and Curtis a graphic account of his discovery of a group of *eykenokhw* at work (Boas 1930:279–81; Curtis 1915:68–70). He threw their gun out of reach before they could use it and quotes one of the witches describing the gun as loaded with "a charge and a half of powder and two bullets . . . a man-load" (Curtis 1915:70).

Sorcerers were said to have a "secret man" accomplice who gathered the material needed from the intended victim. In the film the old Sorcerer sends a message to his daughter calling her to the secret place for instructions. When we first see her she is looking through her jewelry, from which she finally selects a nose ring. The messenger outlines the plot to her and she follows him to the meeting place. There she is instructed by her father to go to where Motana is seeking power and obtain some of his hair and his clothing.

MOTANA HAS AGAIN BUILT HIS FIRE ON THE HEIGHTS WHERE HE FASTS AND DANCES, STILL SEEKING SPIRIT POWER. THE SORCERER'S DAUGHTER RESOLVES TO SPARE HIM AND WIN HIS LOVE, BUT HE SPURNS HER AND SHE RETURNS TO HER FATHER WITH MOTANA'S HAIR AND NECKRING.

Motana climbs the heights and returns to his vigil. He builds his fire, starting it with a hand drill. A tapered stick of very dry cedar is twirled between the hands with its lower end against a cedar board. The friction obtained wears the wood into a hot powder which eventually ignites into a glowing coal. This coal is wrapped in shredded bark and blown on until the bark flames, a laborious and not always successful technique. In the days before flint and steel fire was often kept, even when traveling, by means of a "slow-match," a tightly twisted or wrapped bundle of cedar bark which would smolder a long time.

Motana succeeds in his firebuilding and returns to his dance. His dancing resembles that of a Hamatsa, even to the trembling of his fingers and his pivots to the left at each side of his fire. He lies down by the fire and is soon asleep.

The Sorcerer's daughter, played by Gwikilaokwa (Mrs. George Wal-

kus), approaches Motana and offers to spare him in return for his love. Motana, of course, will have no part of this bargain and sends her away. She reviles him for his rejection of her and goes back to the original plan. As soon as Motana is sound asleep, she takes his neckring and a lock of hair. He seems to be a very heavy sleeper!

When the hero awakes he discovers the loss of his neckring and realizes what has happened. It is important to the success of the witchcraft that the victim know, or at least suspect, that he is being worked on.

THE PLOTTERS, ANTICIPATING MOTANA'S DEATH, "MOURN" HIM AS HIS HAIR, STUFFED IN THE BODIES OF TOADS, SMOKES OVER THEIR FIRE.

Motana's hair and neckring are brought to the sorcerers in the forest. The hair is stuffed into the bodies of toads which are then placed in the split of cooking tongs and smoked over the fire. The witches plan that the heat of the fire will cause Motana to sicken and die.

They begin to "cry for Motana." They sway back and forth and wail in the manner of mourners because they anticipate Motana's death. This follows closely Hunt's descriptions of witchcraft which were published by Curtis and Boas. It is interesting that almost all the detailed descriptions of Kwakiutl sorcery come from George Hunt, who had had many personal experiences with it, according to his accounts.

MOTANA RETURNS TO HIS VILLAGE TO A JOYOUS WELCOME BY HIS TRIBES-MEN.

Having completed his spirit quest Motana returns in his small canoe to his home village. When he is sighted the people rush down to the shore to greet him. They are led by a man who was identified as Bulóotsa, the same actor who plays Naida's father and Yaklus, the old Sorcerer's brother. Probably one of the reasons for the remarkably good acting, considering the lack of formal training of the actors and in relation to the usual motion picture acting of the day, was that Curtis chose only the best for the main parts. In the case of Bulóotsa he relied on costume changes to establish his varying identities. Here he wears a cedar bark (raffia) wrap-around blanket. As Waket he wears a sealskin tunic, and as Yaklus he wears painted hide "armor" and has his hair tied up for war.

As Motana stands in his canoe and approaches the shore, his father Kenada, chief of the village, greets him with a speech of welcome. He stands beside the great Raven entrance pole, holding his "talking stick." Kenada, played by Paddy Maleed, bobs rhythmically and gestures with his stick in the formal oratorical style traditional to the Kwakiutl. The Raven's beak, which opened to be used as an entrance to the house on ceremonial occasions (fig. 30), snaps in rhythm with the speech. This house and its impressive entrance pole were made for the filming of the motion picture. It is in imitation of the large house of Wakyas at Alert Bay. The late Dan Cranmer was the nephew of Wakyas and had the duty, in his youth, of opening and shutting the great beak as each guest entered for a potlatch or feast. Cranmer later moved his own house, which had been built on the hillside behind the pole, to the site of Wakyas' house and the Curtis film was shown there six times when information was being gathered from the Alert Bay people in preparation for the restoration of the movie.

THE JOY OF MOTANA'S RETURN CHANGES TO A CALL FOR WAR WHEN THE WITCHCRAFT OF THE SORCERER IS MADE KNOWN. KENADA AND HIS WARRIORS ATTACK AND DESTROY THE SORCERER AND HIS ASSISTANTS AND BRING THEIR HEADS TO WAKET, NAIDA'S FATHER, ASKING FOR HER MARRIAGE TO MOTANA.

Motana informs his father of the attempt on his life, and of his hope to marry Naida. None of this, nor any of the subsequent war, is seen in the restored film, but the Copyright Office photos show that these scenes were once part of the story. The action can be reconstructed through these photos and Curtis' written versions. Kenada goes to Waket's village (fig. 31) and announces his intent to ask for Naida's hand in marriage to Motana, and promises the Sorcerer's head to Waket. He organizes a war party which attacks the village of the Sorcerer and

kills him and his assistants. Another logical scene would have been a search for, and discovery and nullification of, the witches' work with Motana's hair. Unless this was done Motana would surely have died. Curtis was well aware of this and may very well have included it in his screenplay, but there is no trace of it either in the existing film or in the copyrighted prints.

That the attack on the Sorcerer's village (photographed in Blunden Harbour, fig. 32) was successful is seen by the appearance of Kenada and his warriors paddling into the bay in front of Waket's village. They bring the heads of the Sorcerer and his assistants. This is one of the great scenes of the film, costarring Paddy Maleed and Bulóotsa. Kenada comes to make good his promise to destroy the Sorcerer and to solidify his claim to Naida. He emphasizes his claim by presenting to Waket the head of Naida's former suitor, the old Sorcerer. In this act he demonstrates his own military power, either as an ally or potential enemy, and disposes of the Sorcerer's claim to Naida.

Waket accepts the proposal in a grand flurry of speech and counterspeech. Kenada's style is superb with kneebends and gestures punctuating his speech. The perfect synchronization of the speech rhythm of the film and the soundtrack, made nearly sixty years apart, emphasizes the strength of the Kwakiutl oratorical tradition.

Kenada hands the head of the Sorcerer over to Waket, who proceeds to punch it vigorously, expressing, we suppose, his complete acceptance of the new situation.

WAKET ACCEPTS THE PROPOSAL AND KENADA AND HIS TRIBE COME FOR THE BRIDE IN THEIR GREAT CANOES. THE THUNDERBIRD, THE WASP, AND THE GRIZZLY BEAR DANCE IN THE PROWS.

The tribe of Kenada and Motana prepares to go to "capture" the bride. The great canoes are drawn up at the beach before the village in Deer Island (fig. 33). The boxes of ceremonial material, food, and blankets which will be part of the bride price are loaded. Great animal-form feast dishes are among the goods stowed for the voyage. Finally

30. *Unfortunately the filmed scene showing the guests entering Kenada's house through the Raven's open mouth has been lost, but the Copyright Office photograph proves that it was once part of the motion picture. The concept of a* *devouring mouth as a door of the hosts' house appears in Kwakiutl myths and on this and a number of other house facades with painted or carved creatures with open (or opening) mouths. [LC]*

31. *Much of the film footage dealing with the marriage of Motana and Naida has been lost. Some of these scenes survive only in the prints of single frames of the film submitted by Curtis to the Copyright Office. This picture is an example: Kenada announcing to Waket his intent to claim Waket's daughter Naida as a bride for his son Motana.* [LC]

32. *Kenada and his warriors attack the village of the Sorcerer, in retaliation for the witchcraft worked upon Motana. Kenada also planned to eliminate the Sorcerer as a suitor for Naida's hand. This is another of the sequences that no longer exist in the motion picture film and are preserved only in the copyrighted prints. Curtis utilized the village of Blunden Harbour rather than the imitation village on Deer Island for those scenes which depict the village of the Sorcerer and his brother Yaklus. [LC]*

33. *The great canoes drawn up on the beach of Kenada's village are being loaded for the journey to the village of the bride. The thin, angular cutwaters under the bows of the canoes are easily damaged so canoes were properly landed with the sloping sterns to the beach. Food, ritual paraphernalia, and blankets for the brideprice are carried aboard in bent corner boxes. The large hereditary family feast dishes are also part of the cargo. [Head-Hunters]*

all go aboard. As the flotilla leaves the beach the bridegroom-to-be is seen standing in the canoe, richly dressed in a fur robe and headdress. His father stands behind him holding his valuable copper on his shoulder. The important ceremonial character of the departure of the wedding party is obvious in this scene.

The canoes travel rapidly to their destination, with Thunderbird in the form of a masked dancer in the bow of the leading canoe (fig. 34).

The approach of the wedding party is discovered by a group of young men, whose excitement is apparent. One of them cannot believe his eyes, and splashes his face with water to clear his sight. He is so unnerved by the spectacle that he first forgets his paddle, and then drops it in his bumbling haste. This actor is Bob Wilson, who much later participated in the making of the sound track and contributed a great deal of information about the original filming.

The sight that elicited this wild response produced the most exciting scene in the film, the ceremonial approach of the rafted canoes with masked and costumed figures dancing in the bows (figs. 35 and 36). Grizzly, Thunderbird, and Wasp are represented, displaying the dance privileges of the groom's family. As they approach the village the crews sing war songs, the implication being that they are coming to capture the bride by force. These war songs are still a part of traditional marriage ceremonies.

As the canoes come close to shore the song changes to a dance song, and the three masked figures begin their dances. The spectacular masks and costumes, the great canoes bouncing to the rhythm of paddles struck on the gunwales to mark time, and the dramatic dance movements themselves combine in a scene that epitomizes Kwakiutl ceremonial display. It alone should assure Curtis lasting fame. Grizzly Bear is especially expertly portrayed (fig. 37). A number of people guessed that the dancer was Herbert Martin, a renowned dancer, but he told Bill Holm that he and his older brother Mungo were away at Rivers Inlet during the filming.

KENADA DISTRIBUTES BLANKETS TO THE CHIEFS OF THE BRIDE'S TRIBE, AND HER FATHER LEADS A DANCE OF ACCEPTANCE.

Quite a bit of the detail is missing from the marriage ceremony depicted in the film, as can be seen from the copyright photograph (fig. 38). What is shown is the counting out of the blankets to be paid the bride's father. The custom has been described frequently in the literature (see, for example, Boas 1925:271–73), and is very much abbreviated in the film. The blankets, in keeping with the precontact setting of the story, are native-made rather than Hudson's Bay Company blankets, which formed the bulk of such payments during the late nineteenth and early twentieth centuries. Of course many of the blankets passed out in this scene were made of the raffia furnished by Curtis to Tsukwani (Mrs. George Hunt) and others.

Naida's father then leads a dance of acceptance (fig. 39). Most informants identified this as *umlala*, "play dance." Its significance here is not certain. The participants have been identified as Bulóotsa of Blunden Harbour as Waket; Yakhyugidzumga, also of Blunden Harbour, known as a famous dancer; Gwikimgilakw (Emily Hunt Wilson), daughter of George Hunt and mother of Mrs. Frank, Mrs. Knox and Bob Wilson; Tlakwagilayookwa (Sara Smith Hunt, later Martin), George Hunt's daughter-in-law at the time, here playing Naida; Paddy Maleed as Kenada; and the drummer A'widi of Blunden Harbour. The woman at the side of the house leading women dancing is Mrs. George Hunt.

A CONTEST OF DRINKING CANDLEFISH OIL DEVELOPS BETWEEN THE SPEAKERS OF THE TWO CHIEFS, AND THE DANCE PRIVILEGES TO BE GIVEN IN THE DOWRY ARE DISPLAYED.

Rivalry between two chiefs is expressed in many ways. The version chosen by Curtis is the grease-eating contest. Here the speakers of the two chiefs vie with one another in drinking the rendered oil of the candlefish. The wooden figure set up near the fire represents the rival who is being ridiculed. Grease (as the oil is called in English) is fed to

34. *The Thunderbird dancer "flying" in the bow of the canoe is one of the most spectacular images in the collection. It has been utilized as the opening sequence in the reconstructed film. The dancer's body as completely covered with eagle skins and feathers. This costume was probably made of the eagle skins acquired by George Hunt for the film. [Curtis]*

35. *The dance of Grizzly Bear, Thunderbird and Wasp is certainly the most popular scene in the reconstructed film. Spectacularly masked and costumed dancers perform in the bows of the canoes of the groom's party as they approach the village of the bride's father. The scene is well known through its publication as one of the plates accompanying volume 10 of* The North American Indian. *This snapshot by Edmund Schwinke shows a slightly different version. [Schwinke]*

36. *The special value of the Schwinke photographs lies in the information they furnish about off-camera activities. Here the unmasked Wasp dancer disembarks from the canoe. The platforms on which the dancers perform can be seen here resting across the gunwales.* [Schwinke]

37. *The Grizzly Bear dancer is the most impressive of the three in the film. These dances are more than just spectacular display. They illustrate inherited privileges of the groom's family, and make his nobility more apparent to the watching tribesmen of the bride. [Schwinke]*

38. The transfer of a copper from the bride's father to the groom's father is an important incident in a noble marriage. Here Waket holds his big copper while his speaker, with his talking stick, announces Waket's intent to the guests. Naida (here Mrs. David Hunt) sits demurely between them. This scene no longer appears in the film as it is today. [LC]

39. (facing page) Waket, his daughter Naida, and members of their retinue perform a dance as part of the wedding ceremony. The painted boxlike object held by the man seated at the right is a drum. Made of a single large cedar plank kerfed and bent to form the four sides and with another plank pegged on to close the end, it was beaten with the fist. [Curtis]

the image as if he doesn't have any of his own. The arguing and taunting shown so dramatically in the film are all part of the show. They may not have any real rancor behind them at all. Drinking, wasting, and burning quantities of the valuable oil were means of displaying wealth.

The use of grease as a food is still common today; most Indian families in the area prize and use it, and it is becoming more valuable all the time. A particularly prestigious act is to give large quantities away in what is called a "grease feast." In 1948 at such an occasion, six hundred five-gallon cans of candlefish oil were distributed by one chief. The dances that are to be transferred at the wedding are shown. In the Curtis film the dance performed is called *noontlum*. This is one of the important ritual dances of the Nákwakhdakhw and Quatsino people. In the dance a group of pierced and painted panels made of thin split boards (now in the Burke Museum) are made to rise above a screen of crouching dancers (fig. 40). The boards are ingeniously joined so they can be made to seem to grow taller and taller, swaying as they grow, and then to disappear slowly, apparently into the ground. They are spotted with bits of mica glued to their surfaces, which sparkle in the firelight. The panels, called *duntsik*, are said to represent the three-headed serpent Sisiutl, and the performance is called *hyilkhtsayoo*, or "means of harm." This signifies that anyone who sees the being will die or be harmed. Curtis paid thirty dollars for the set, or five dollars per panel for the *duntsik* boards.

MOTANA AND NAIDA RETURN WITH POMP TO KENADA'S VILLAGE, BUT YAK-LUS, BROTHER OF THE SLAIN SORCERER, LEARNS OF HIS BROTHER'S DEATH AND GOES TO WAR FOR REVENGE. HE ATTACKS WHOMEVER HE MEETS, FIRST A PARTY OF FISHERMEN AND THEN A GROUP OF CLAM DIGGERS.

The return of the bridal couple to Kenada's village was filmed but has been lost (fig. 41). In the meantime the war chief Yaklus, brother of the Sorcerer who was killed by Kenada, has vowed to avenge his brother's death (figs. 42 and 43). No one is safe from such a war party. Both Curtis and Boas have published accounts of the activities of war

parties that agree with the film version. The idea that revenge could be carried out on anyone the warriors met, and that these victims might be innocent fishermen, clam diggers, or travelers surprised almost all non-Indians who saw and commented on the film during the time we were gathering information on it. Older Kwakiutl viewers were generally aware of the war customs of their ancestors and were not surprised or shocked by the action.

A misleading statement related to war customs is seen in the caption of one of the illustrations in the 1915 article "Filming the Head-Hunters" (Appendix 4). A photograph of Bulóotsa holding several "heads" (similar to Schwinke's photo, fig. 25) is captioned "Valslus [a misprint of Yaklus], the most famous member of the head-hunting band of the North Pacific Coast. Valslus is now a very peaceable Indian since head-hunting has been suppressed." Bulóotsa, the famous headhunter, was probably not yet born when the last heads were taken in war by the Kwakiutl.

Yaklus leads his warriors against a fishing party in a small canoe. One man, with his hair tied up and armed with a dagger, leads the actual attack by leaping on the capsizing canoe and striking the crewmen with his stone weapon. He is probably a "warrior" *(ba'bak'wa)* as opposed to a "crewman." Such men were trained for fighting and were said to be always surly and aggressive.

The attack on the clam diggers illustrates a number of interesting points. As Yaklus and his warriors approach the beach, the unsuspecting women are busy digging. They put their clams in openwork twined baskets of a type still in occasional use by the Kwakiutl, even when digging commercially. They are so perfectly functional that they have never been entirely superseded by any modern counterpart. When the diggers see the warriors it is too late to escape, but they run in panic. The canoes are driven straight onto the beach, but are immediately reversed, almost before the attacking warriors are clear. Canoes ordinarily were beached stern first because the vertical cutwater at the bow is easily damaged by striking rock or gravel, while the sloping stern tends to ride over them. Poles are used in landing and moving big canoes in shallow water.

40. *The power boards, or duntsik, used in the Noontlum ceremony as they appear in the film. One of the greatest ethnological values of the Curtis film is in the depiction of objects in use that are known to most people today only as artifacts in museums or as pictures or descriptions in books. The pierced and painted boards are constructed in such a way that they can be joined together to grow taller and taller and then recede with an undulating motion. They represent a supernatural being, probably the Sisiutl, and are described as being dangerous to look at. [Schwinke]*

41. *The pageant of the return of the bridal party to the groom's village is preserved in this plate from* The North American Indian. *Unfortunately it is another of the scenes that were lost in the film itself. The bride and groom stand in a decorated settee placed across the gunwales of the canoe while a dancer performs in the bow. [Curtis]*

42. *Yaklus leads his warriors on a raid for revenge. He exhorts them to be ruthless to his brother's killers and to whomever else they might meet. This scene was also shot at Blunden Harbour and shows the elevated boardwalk along the front of the village. Yaklus was said to have been played by the same man who acted the part of Waket. In the part of the war chief he wears a painted hide tunic and has his hair tied in back, which serve to distinguish him from Waket. [LC]*

43. *Schwinke's photograph of the warriors on the beach at Blunden Harbour catches them lining up in preparation for shooting the scene. Their relaxed postures suggest the ease with which the Kwakiutl participants handled the actor's role. [Schwinke]*

The warriors soon return with heads and slaves. The small captive girl was played by Helen Wilson Knox, another of George Hunt's granddaughters, and a participant in the restoration of the film. An interesting point of realism which sets Curtis' opus apart from almost all modern adventure films is the gathering up of the clam diggers' discarded equipment by the departing warriors. As the canoes race out over the bay with booty and slaves aboard, Yaklus gestures triumphantly with a trophy head and his dagger, the same dagger used earlier by Kenada, and now in the Burke Museum.

A party of travelers flees the terrible warriors. They drive their small canoe against a bank and scramble hurriedly up. They would have had no chance to outrun the fifty-foot war canoe with its powerful crew. Almost immediately the great canoe appears around the point. The warriors work their huge craft around the rock, bending the shafts of their paddles against the gunwales. It is pictures such as these, illustrating canoe handling techniques still known in 1914, that make Curtis' film so valuable as an ethnographic record.

The warriors in turn scramble up the rocks in pursuit of the luckless travelers. Yaklus himself meets one of them in hand to hand combat. The two figures struggle to the brink of the cliff. Finally Yaklus frees his right arm and strikes his adversary with his whalebone club, then hurls him into the sea.

One of the apparent losses in the damage to the original film by fire and deterioration was the inevitable conclusion of this struggle. The unedited film left Yaklus and his victim struggling on the brink. Kwakiutl who viewed it invariably asked about the missing action. The making of the dummy, its "death," and fall into the sea were well known even to people too young to have witnessed the filming personally. David Hunt's failure to weight the legs properly, which allowed the "dead man" to bob quickly to the surface, was remembered with humor. Even Edward Curtis laughed, although many participants recall him as "cranky," in that he was a perfectionist. No modern clothes could show, for example, and several people whose white ancestry was too evident

were not allowed to participate, and so on. The missing "death" of the dummy could not be tolerated. It is the one bit of action film added to Curtis' original work. A dummy was constructed of wire, old mattress covers and stuffing, and a wig. Painted and dressed in a burlap imitation of a cedar-bark robe, he looked the part silhouetted atop an appropriate cliff. Channing Bartlett doubled for Yaklus in the final struggle. The dummy was back in the film. Schwinke's photograph of Yaklus looking down over the cliff and the photograph of the dummy in a boat with Curtis and Schwinke preserve the only record we have found of the fight's climax (figs. 44 and 45).

The excitement and great enjoyment that the people felt in reconstructing their old ways continually comes out in conversations with the old people who participated in that adventure. Edmund Schwinke's photographs have preserved some of the off-camera shenanigans that illustrate the lighter sides of Kwakiutl life glimpsed only fleetingly in the film itself. Teenage warriors resting in their great canoe between takes parody the violence of the story (figs. 46 and 47). "Cranky" Edward Curtis swings on a platform railing in Blunden Harbour while Kwakiutl actors lightheartedly display the imitation heads, one of them under a spruce-root hat (fig. 48).

FINALLY YAKLUS ATTACKS KENADA'S VILLAGE (FIG. 49). IN THE BLOODY BATTLE THE OLD CHIEF IS SLAIN AND NAIDA TAKEN CAPTIVE. MOTANA ESCAPES, WOUNDED, WITH A HANDFUL OF HIS TRIBESMEN.

The climax of Yaklus' war of revenge is his attack on Kenada's village. It was intended to be depicted as a night attack, and perhaps the hand-tinting of the film expressed this. The warriors quietly paddle around the point and land on the beach. Scouts leap ashore and creep up to the silent houses. They check and discover the occupants are asleep. The warriors are summoned and surround the village and the attack begins. Again parts of this action are missing, most notably the capture of Naida and the wounding of Motana. Kenada's death is shown, the old chief escaping his house through the ceremonial door in Raven's

44. *Yaklus and his men attack anyone they come upon, according to the custom of warriors. After a violent hand-to-hand struggle he kills an unfortunate traveler with his whale-bone club and hurls the body over a cliff into the sea. The finale of this fight is missing from the film, but the Schwinke photograph shows Yaklus gazing after his victim. [Schwinke]*

45. *The "victim" which Yaklus hurled off the cliff was a dummy, remembered well by Kwakiutl participants in the film. The Schwinke photographs preserve the only relic of this incident. Here Curtis sits in the stern of a dinghy with the dummy stretched across the gunwales in front of him, while Schwinke maneuvers from the bow with a paddle. The dinghy was being towed by a large canoe from which the photograph was taken. We can only guess who the photographer was, perhaps George Hunt. For the reconstruction of the film a new dummy was made based on the recollections of the Kwakiutl participants, and the newly photographed scene was inserted at the conclusion of the fight on the cliff. [Schwinke]*

46. *Schwinke's Kodak captures some levity during the filming. Yaklus' savage warriors turn out to be boys having a lot of fun. This photograph is also interesting in that it is a seldom-seen view of a big Northwest Coast canoe with the paddlers and their equipment aboard. [Schwinke]*

47. *Another break in filming finds the warriors relaxing on a small beach. This view of the large canoes well illustrates their elegant lines. The little cluster of figures beyond the tripod in the background includes Curtis and George Hunt.* [Schwinke]

48. *Edward S. Curtis and his hobnailed boots swing on the railing at Blunden Harbour. Schwinke's camera has caught another lighthearted moment during the making of the film. Although Curtis has a reputation as a strict taskmaster in the recollections of the Indian participants, this picture shows that he was able to put aside that role. The Kwakiutl actors also clown for Schwinke's camera. Here one of the "trophy heads" has been crowned with a spruce-root hat. [Schwinke]*

49. *The warriors make a night attack on Kenada's village. Many of the war scenes, such as this one, are now missing from the film. Some of the copyright prints show "bodies" of the victims, interior shots with fallen and charred beams, and other evidence of the violent attack.* [LC]

beak and bravely parrying arrows with his club until he falls. Yaklus directs the final attack of his archers and spearsmen. The predawn attack on sleeping villagers, the firing of the houses, simulated by smoke pots and coloring of the film (fig. 50), and the capture of slaves are all features of old Kwakiutl warfare. The "bloodthirsty" warriors are seen resting on the beach in Schwinke's photograph (figs. 51 and 52).

THE PEOPLE OF YAKLUS' VILLAGE ARE GAMBLING WHEN THE WARRIORS ARE SIGHTED RETURNING WITH HEADS AND BOOTY. THEY BOAST OF THEIR TROPHIES IN A DANCE.

Again Curtis inserts another custom which has little to do with the story. The people play at the well-known gambling game *slahal,* called by the Kwakiutl *lehal* or *álakhwa.* The game is widespread in the Northwest and is still very popular among Salish and Sahaptian people. The Kwakiutl seldom play today. Curtis' picture is somewhat misleading. Apparently he felt he could not clearly show the characteristic action of the game with the players in the traditional parallel facing rows, so he spread them into a single line with only one player on the near team (fig. 53).

A lookout arrives to announce the return of the warriors, and the game breaks up. The players cluster on a point gesturing toward the approaching canoes.

The victorious warriors beach their canoe and the trophy heads and captive slaves are passed ashore. Yaklus is seen for the first time wearing a cedar-bark neckring of the type worn by participants in the Winter Ceremonial, probably indicating that the killing of enemies has activated his *leyda,* or dance privilege. Boas concluded (1897:664) that the "secret societies" had their origin in war customs, and almost all detailed descriptions of Kwakiutl warfare tend to show a relationship between the two. Warriors who belong to the higher and more aggressive dances get excited when they kill an enemy and act as if possessed by their motivating spirit.

As a woman, presumably his wife, takes heads from him, Yaklus places a neckring over her head too, strengthening the supposition that the Winter Ceremony has come into effect. The women carrying the heads up the beach make a ceremonial pivot just as they would in the Winter Dance. Yaklus himself makes the pivot as he comes up the beach. These actions could also be explained by considering that Yaklus had acquired a dance by killing its owner, probably Kenada, in the war. Either explanation is acceptable.

The warriors then perform a dance of boasting, in which each brandishes a wreath of hemlock boughs for every head he has taken (fig. 54). Only a very few people recognized the significance of the action; war customs are a thing of the remote past. Joe Seaweed, of Blunden Harbour, on seeing the film showing Yaklus with a wreath in each hand remarked, "I guess he's got two heads." Both Curtis (1915:105) and Boas (1921:1364–66) describe the custom. The two descriptions are similar and resemble closely the action seen in the film except that Curtis describes it as an incident in the Winter Ceremonial in which warriors vie with one another in boasting of the heads they have taken, while Boas explains it as the warriors pledging to take heads in an ensuing war. George Hunt was probably the source for each version. In the film, it is plain that the warriors are boasting of heads taken.

THE KILLING OF ENEMIES BRINGS ON THE WINTER CEREMONIAL POWER OF THE WARRIORS. THE CEREMONY OF FIRST-APPEARANCE-OF-MASKS-IN-THE-HOUSE IS FOLLOWED BY THE PERFORMANCE OF THE MASKED DANCERS.

The display of masks by lowering a curtain was called *gílsgumlihla* by all Indian viewers who called it by name. Boas (1921:1179) and Curtis (1915:171) used the term *húkhsumlihla* to designate the performance. Again the two descriptions differ as to the place of the ritual in the ceremonial setting. Curtis' description matches closely the idea that present-day Kwakiutl have about it, that it is a display of the masks to be used at the ensuing Winter Ceremonial, shown just before the new dance initiates are taken away by the motivating spirits.

The first masked dancer to appear is the Grouse man. This is very

50. *During the attack Kenada's village is burned. Kwakiutl participants remember the smoky fires that were lighted to simulate the destruction of the village. In the original 35mm film some of these scenes were dyed with a reddish color to represent the fire.* [Head-Hunters]

51. *Between takes, the cast and filmmakers rest on the beach in front of the Deer Island village. Schwinke's candid photograph captured the casual atmosphere of the scene. [Schwinke]*

52. *Yaklus' fierce warriors, now aware of the photographer, mug for the camera.*
Edward Curtis and friends can be seen near the far corner of the house. [Schwinke]

53. *The game of* lehal *in progress in Yaklus' village before the return of the victorious warriors. The arrangement of the players in this popular gambling game was altered by Curtis, apparently to show more clearly the action of the gamblers. In the actual game there are two parallel rows of players facing each other.* [Curtis]

54. *Dancing around the fire after their triumphant return, the warriors brandish
hemlock wreaths symbolizing the heads they have taken in their raids.* [LC]

curious, because the Grouse man acts as the one who calls out the dancers in a festival called *atla'k!em*, which is quite different from *gílsgumlihla*. In the film he dances exactly like the caller for *atla'k!em*. It seems unlikely that Curtis could have induced the Indians to mix up two unrelated ceremonies. No one today is able to explain it. The singers beat time on boxes, another old custom. At each side of the curtain can be seen attendants who always accompany the dancers.

The showing of all the masks so briefly before the dances begin is anticipated by the Indian audience in the dance house. Dancers shouting over the sound of the box-beating and rattles, masks moving, beaks snapping, combine in a striking display that disappears as quickly as it appears. The audience is tantalized. What mask was that? What did that one do? In the real ceremony the curtain is dropped once more and another, too short, glimpse is available. The masks and dancers seen behind the curtain are of many types. The large bird masks with snapping beaks are like those of the *hamatsa* ceremony, although this type of mask is also used in the *atla'k!em* ceremony. A large whale "back-mask" displays a fin, which suddenly fans into an arc of segments. An animal head mask splits and springs open, revealing a humanoid face inside. A woman dancing in place with springing movement emphasized by fluttering eagle feathers attached to her blanket is Nu'nalalahl, the weather dancer. One with a wolf forehead mask and thumbs raised from clenched fists is Dloogwala ("obtaining a treasure"), the wolf dancer. Hanging suspended against the wall and gesturing dramatically are two figures. They are *háwinalahl*, "war dancers." They are supposed to be hanging from thongs attached through slits in the skin of the shoulder blades and thighs. (How this was done for the movie is suggested by Myer's letter to Schwinke, chap. 3, p. 28.) Their power gives them insensitivity to pain. The last real Háwinalahl was hung up around the turn of the century, a decade and a half before Curtis filmed this scene, but the dance was well remembered.

The dancers are then shown dancing in a circle. The scene is spectacular, but leaves much to be explained. It apparently expresses Curtis'

intent to show all the masks in action, as no modern informant has been able to explain the juxtaposition of all these masks in one dance. Participants remember Curtis drawing a circle on the floor, apparently to guide the dancers to stay in camera range.

The quality of dancing is mixed. This may be due partly to the artificial situation in which the dancers found themselves. It is difficult to dance to a song and a beat that doesn't belong to one's own dance. Outstanding are the Bukwus dancer in the center of the circle, the weather dancer with feathered robe, and the sleepy Dzoonokwa in the background beside the housepost.

The outstanding dance sequence is the performance by Thunderbird (fig. 55). Alone and displayed before a plain curtain, the bird, completely covered with feathers and mask, poses, preens, prances, and soars. The scene was much admired by Indian audiences—an excellent example of Kwakiutl dramatization of the mythic bird.

A spectacular scene, which was photographed (fig. 56) but which has not survived in the film, is a great gathering of these same costumed dancers on a trimaran made by laying planks across three canoes.

THE FIRE DANCER DESTROYS THE FIRE WITH BARE HANDS, WHILE HIS ATTENDANTS TRY TO RESTRAIN HIM. THE BEAR, WOLF, MOUNTAIN GOAT, WASP, DOG, AND DEER PERFORM.

The Noónsistalahl, or "fireman" as he is called in English today, is imbued by his spirit power with a compulsion to destroy the fire. His attendants try to prevent him from getting at it, but he always manages to elude them and scatters the burning sticks around the house. The film was made out of doors, but the dance is properly done in the house, where the reckless throwing of the blazing logs in showers of sparks and the gradual darkening of the house as the fire is extinguished is unforgettably dramatic.

The animals, this time Bear, Wolf, Mountain Goat, Wasp, Dog, and Deer, dance again. This performance is no more easily explained than the other mass dance. Perhaps it is meant to be a dance of the

55. *In the dance festival following the return of the victorious warriors, the Thunderbird performs a dramatic dance. He stands posed with wings spread in Curtis' still photograph, but in the film he wheels, darts, preens and shudders like a great, supernatural bird. [Curtis]*

56. *Another dramatic scene, lost to the film, is shown in a series of Schwinke photographs. A platform built across three canoes is crowded with masked dancers of all sorts. These are the same dancers who appear in the great festival in Yaklus' house, so we can guess that this scene was intended to be part of that sequence. [Schwinke]*

animals, similar to the *atla'k!em*, dramatizing the story of the discovery by an ancestor of the animals' dancing house.

NAIDA'S SLAVE ESCAPES FROM YAKLUS' VILLAGE AND, ALTHOUGH WOUNDED BY AN ARROW, MAKES HIS WAY TO MOTANA. HEARING THAT NAIDA HAS SURVIVED, HE AND HIS WARRIORS PADDLE TO HER RESCUE.

Missing from the film here is the escape of Naida's slave from captivity in Yaklus' village. He bears a token from Naida and a plea for rescue to be taken to Motana, who has recovered from his wounds and has assembled a band of survivors. The messenger is wounded during his escape, but manages to steal a canoe and paddle to Motana's camp.

The messenger gives his token, perhaps a personal article of Naida's that Motana would recognize, and then collapses on the beach. Motana assembles his warriors and calls for help in rescuing his wife. A canoe is quickly launched, while Motana draws the arrow from the slave's wound. His sudden recovery and apparent eagerness to accompany the rescue expedition were viewed with amusement by Indian audiences.

REACHING YAKLUS' VILLAGE, MOTANA RESCUES HIS WIFE. YAKLUS PURSUES THEM AND FOLLOWS MOTANA'S CANOE INTO A SURGING GORGE WHERE HIS CANOE CAPSIZES AND HE AND HIS WARRIORS DROWN.

The hero and his crew reach Yaklus' village and land quietly. Motana leaves his comrades in the canoe and creeps up the steps which lead from the beach to the village street (fig. 57). The villagers are asleep; it is probably just before dawn. This scene was shot at Blunden Harbour, where similar steps still join the beach and the village level.

Motana cautiously opens the door of Yaklus' house and slips inside. Naida, in the meantime, has awakened and decides to take the opportunity to kill her sleeping captor Yaklus. She finds his double-bladed dagger and approaches the warchief, dagger poised. At that moment she hears the approaching Motana and together they flee the house. This Naida is Margaret Frank, with long hair contrasting with the shorter cut of the Naida of the following scene, played by Mrs. George Walkus.

Yaklus awakes, finds his captive gone, and angrily calls his warriors. They rush out of the house after the fleeing couple who have raced down the beach and hurriedly boarded their canoe. The crewmen push off and begin their wild dash for safety.

The pursuing warriors and their chief find the marks of the canoe in the beach. They drag a fast canoe to the water and set off recklessly in pursuit. The casualness with which a half dozen or so people jump into a small canoe and race out across choppy Beaver Harbour, one of them standing in the middle waving his arms, is startling!

The film climaxes with a wild canoe chase. The hero and his rescued bride, with their faithful canoemen, bend their paddles in desperate effort to outdistance the overtaking canoe of fierce warriors. Slowly the pursuers shorten the gap. The two canoes fairly leap out of the water with the stroke of the paddles. The deteriorated image on the film, with its wild shimmering splotches, seems to enhance the feeling of desperate struggle.

Yaklus' warriors have almost closed with the fleeing canoe when Motana takes a last desperate gamble and orders his steersman to bring the boat through a fearful surging gorge. The paddlers summon all their strength and skill to navigate the wild waters. Yaklus boldly follows, but his canoe broaches and capsizes, throwing the warriors into the sea. They all drown and their bodies roll in the surf. Motana's canoe rides in the calm waters beyond the gorge as the film ends.

This scene was believed to have been filmed near Cape Scott, where heavy swells occur.

57. *Motana creeps up to Yaklus' house to rescue his wife. Like many scenes in the film, this one was probably supposed to take place at night, but Curtis was unable to achieve that effect in filming. Still it is a dramatic scene of the* *young hero stealthily entering his enemy's house. Many Kwakiutl villages, built on middens or on natural terraces above the beach, had steps like this one.* *[LC]*

VII. The Afterword: 1915–52

The motion picture was a great disappointment to Edward Curtis. Despite the acclaim of movie critics and the enthusiastic acceptance by people of letters and science, *In the Land of the Head-Hunters* was not a financial success. Curtis and his stockholders had expected large monetary returns on their investment; as it turned out they never got any money.

Curtis had not lived at home in Seattle for many years. He was either in the field or in the East. Since at least 1911 his office for The North American Indian Inc. had been in New York City and he had not been active in the Curtis studio in Seattle since 1904 when Adolph Muhr took over the operation.

By 1915 Curtis seemed clearly headed for divorce. He spent a tremendous amount of time on the affairs of the North American Indian Inc., and seemed barely interested in the Curtis Studio in Seattle. Ella McBride and Edmund Schwinke got wind of this and attempted to purchase the studio. On 21 December 1914 Schwinke wrote to Curtis, then living at the Hotel Belmont in New York.

Dear Chief: Miss McBride tells me that Beth [Curtis] said something to her of your feeling that you would like to discontinue the Studio, if it were not for the sentiment attached to it. . . . Miss McBride and I have talked things over, and we would like to make you a proposition in view of taking it off your hands. If some such arrangement as I will suggest could be entered into, it would relieve you of all the bother, and at the same time would give us a profit. . . . The Studio business need not take any more of my time than it has of yours, and I could continue working for you [on *The North American Indian*] as at present.

Curtis apparently did not accept their offer to take over the Studio, although he was engaged in other matters, such as planning for a new series of motion picture. The volume on the Kwakiutl was published in 1915 and Curtis was also busy taking care of his subscribers. In the Burke Museum archives there is a letter written on 22 April 1915 from the Curtis office in New York which shows how Curtis took care of his subscribers and also what he thought of his publication. In the cover letter to volume 10 and portfolio of *The North American Indian*, addressed to Lawrence J. Colman in Seattle, he wrote:

I feel that this volume is in many respects worthy of special consideration. The Indian life of the region covered presents many unique and even startling phases. These hardy, sea-going people had developed the ceremonial life until it was a veritable pageant. It is, perhaps, safe to say that nowhere else in North America had the natives developed so far towards a distinctive drama. . . . Strange as it may seem, the further the coast tribes had developed in culture which tended towards civilization and the greater their vigor, the more pronounced their warfare and the taking of heads. The poor and lowly tribes could scarce risk war raids, whereas the more powerful and aggressive tribes, rich in canoes and slaves, could well take the hazard of warfare and thus add further to the wealth of their chiefs, by securing more slaves, and, at the same time, add to their tribal standing by the taking of heads. As you will see by the text of the volume, slavery was an important institution.

No volume of the series has required an equal amount of labor in the collecting of data, and in few places have I been so fortunate in securing information needed. . . . The pageant-like ceremonies of the life, their great canoes and ocean-shore homeland, have afforded rare material for pictures. Again, their rich ceremonial life combined with their skill in carving and fertile imagination in the designing of ceremonial paraphernalia, furnishes costume material not found elsewhere.

Quite aside from the extraordinary features of the volume, I feel that it occupies an unusual position, in that it is the half-way goal in our undertaking. I believe any subscriber of the work will share in the feeling of satisfaction.

In addition to his work for The North American Indian Inc., Curtis had written two books, *Indian Days of the Long Ago* (1914) and *In the Land of the Head-Hunters* (1915), which was based on the scenario of his 1914 motion picture. Curtis also had plans for a number of new motion pictures from which he expected profits. On 22 February 1915 he wrote of his plans to Edmund Schwinke:

Dear Schwinke: I wish you would immediately shape up your books and other affairs in Seattle so as to be able to leave on the shortest possible notice. I may ask you to go into the field and do a month's motion picture work and scenic stuff. That is, going out quite by yourself, and instructions will probably come by wire, so lose no time in getting everything in such shape that you can pull out for a trip of a month or six weeks.

I will probably have you use the motor camera. Please see our repair man and learn if the Pathe Camera can be adjusted to conform to register with our motor camera. It may require the making of a new appateur plate. Of course, if I decide to use this camera for some work, I will purchase a new lens and mount. I think it is in good shape aside from the fact that the present lens is worthless. In case I wire you I will have film shipped to meet you and general instructions by mail at your point of work. Yours, E. S. C.

By 4 May 1915, Curtis' plans for motion pictures were fairly specific. He crowded his schedule for a "picture tour of the beauty spots of America" with a proposed motion picture a week for fifty-two weeks. He notified Schwinke of the schedule:

Dear Schwinke, As far as I can see at the moment, I will have you join me at the Grand Canyon about the 24th. . . .

Among the different items which I want you to bring are:

The motor camera and its accompanying equipment.

Both motion picture tripods. Have old one given any repairs needed, and if I am right, there is no tilting head to it. I am presuming that such is the case and unless I get a wire from you saying that there is a tilting head, I will purchase one and bring it with me.

The small red dark tent.

The 6 x 8 camera and accompanying holders, etc. Have cardboard cut for all holders, in order that I can use cut films in them.

One small brown tent.

Light blanket equipment for yourself, no blanket or bedding for me. You will probably have but one or two periods in camp on the present trip and we will undoubtedly get back to Seattle within six weeks from your starting.

You will not need your typewriter, nor do I think you will need your books and files. We will take a chance at least on leaving them at Seattle.

If possible, in the time at your disposal, try to get color screen for your motion camera lens.

We will first be making a thousand foot motion picture of Grand Canyon. I will work with you a few days in starting it and then leave you to finish. You will next join me at Yosemite and there you will have two or three days with me and again it will be up to you to finish the picture.

My plans are just for the present somewhat confidential, but I am starting a picture tour of the beauty spots of America to be covered in still pictures, as well as motion photography. It will be fifty-two weeks of a scenic picture a week. The stills are to be published in Leslie's, and the motion pictures going through motion picture channels. After leaving you at the Yellowstone, I return to Albuquerque and join a Congressional party there, covering certain conservation projects in Arizona, New Mexico, through California, Nevada, Colorado, Oregon, Washington, Montana and Idaho. You will touch with me when our party is in the Yosemite. . . .

I must find a camera man somewhere in the west that can help me in this undertaking for a few months. Will you look up Hudson and see what he is doing and learn whether he would care to consider a few months work? If he is not available, ask Dobbs if he knows of anyone. The man would have to be able to make both motion and do still work. Yours, ESC

This letter brought an immediate, if unexpected, response from Schwinke, who sent Curtis a telegram followed by a letter of resignation dated 13 May 1915.

Dear Chief: This is an explanation of my telegram of today.

The immediate reason for my decision to leave is that the proposed undertaking described in your letter does not appeal to me, and further, I do not feel that I am qualified to make the sort of pictures that would be expected. Not having had any definite word from you in regard to anything during the past winter, I did not seem until now to be in a position to determine whether it was time to leave or not.

The heart of the matter is that I simply cannot afford to stay longer. I have put in over five years at this work, and have not got anywhere, and am probably less fitted to hold down the ordinary, everyday sort of a position than I was when I started. It is time for me to change, and this seems to be the time for making the change.

I hope that my leaving will not inconvenience you to any great extent. I hardly feel that it will, if I have surmised rightly what your plans are. In fact, I rather think my leaving will be to your advantage. The work I have been doing the past couple of years could as well have been done by a man who was paid a great deal less.

At the end of the month I will send Mr. Albert my North American Indian salary statements for April and May. Please instruct him to have Mr. Pegram take care of them, and also those statements that are already in his hands.

I do not know what you will be able to do at present about the amount I have coming from the film company for services and expenditures. You will of course take care of that. Further, I also feel that you are under obligation to make good the amount I put into the film stock. It was done by me after considerable urging on your part, and I suppose was partly at least for the purpose of enabling you to tell prospective purchasers of stock that your helpers had seen the value of it and had purchased some. When I learn where I can reach you by letter I will send you a statement covering the film company matter.

I want to assure you that there is no ill feeling toward you. We have evidently simply come to the parting of the ways. Sincerely yours,

These letters and others to follow indicate that *In the Land of the Head-Hunters* was a failure financially, that Schwinke was owed money for salary and expenses by the Seattle Film Company,[1] and that

1. Apparently by 1914 the Continental Film Company had become the Seattle Film Company. The Moore Theater handbill of 7–15 December 1914 lists the Seattle Film Co., Inc., as the producer of *In the Land of the Head-Hunters* presented by the World Film Corporation. Mrs. Robert Flaherty recorded in her diary (9 April 1915) that Curtis' motion picture was being handled by the World Film Co. on a 50–50 royalty basis with 26 copies routed (Jay Ruby 1979, personal communication). This information was given Mrs. Flaherty by someone in the Curtis studio, but not by Edward Curtis himself. Schwinke lists expenses and salary in account with Seattle Film Company beginning 1 January 1914 through 31 May 1915 (Burke Museum Archives).

his investment in the film company stock had not paid off. According to a carbon copy of Schwinke's account sent to Curtis on 31 May 1915, Schwinke had not been paid since the end of August 1914; he was owed $461.14. But it was not only money that bothered Schwinke. He was tired of motion picture photography. "I have had enough of that to last me three lifetimes," he wrote to Myers. Schwinke's three lifetimes had been spent in operating the motion picture camera in the production of *In the Land of the Head-Hunters* the previous year.

Within several days of receiving Schwinke's telegram of resignation Curtis sent him two cables: one expressing his regret at the resignation, with instructions for Schwinke to send the motion picture camera to the Cosmos Club in Washington, D.C., and the other requesting that all the bookkeeping files and film be sent to the New York office and asking for information on a substitute cameraman. Then on 22 May he wrote:

Dear Schwinke: Since receiving your letter I have been too busy even to write.

Mr. Albert will be able to get you North American Indian checks from Pegram when statements come in. As to the Film Company items, I will have to manage to take care of that later. There is no money whatever in the Film Company's treasury at this time and as to the matter of your stock, I will do the best I can in view of caring for it. The picture *In the Land of the Head Hunters* will win out alright in time and give us our money back, but just now it is certainly not a producing asset. I will look out for your interest the best I can.

I am more than sorry that you have found it necessary to take up other work. However, we all have to do the best we can for ourselves. I am wondering if you will be in Seattle if I reach there some time towards the end of next month.

Schwinke replied, sending two pages of explanation of his bookkeeping system, the cash-books, journals, and ledgers.

Dear Chief: I have now finished the bookkeeping, and am sending in a box by Northern Express, the following: North American Indian cash-book, journal, and ledgers, Film Company cash-book, journal, stock journal and stock ledger (all in one book), and ledger, and your personal books (cash-book, journal and ledger in one cover). Also North American Indian receipts, Film Co. receipts, and personal receipts. I think this will be all it will be necessary for you to have at present. Sending complete files by express would be quite an item. If you do need anything else, let me know.

The box also contains various financial and tax statements which it will be necessary for the bookkeeper to refer to at times. Also the rewind for the motor camera.

I want to thank you for your letter of the 22nd regarding money coming to me. I am sending Mr. Albert the statements. I also attach statement in account with the Film Company.

I will probably be in Seattle at least six or eight weeks, if I leave at all. I haven't attempted to look around for something else. I think I will just loaf and rest up for a couple of weeks.

Hudson has an Urban motion camera, using films in 150 ft. lengths. The aperture corresponds with that of the motor camera. He also has 6½ x 8½ plate tripod camera, and 5 x 7 graflex.

Will write again in a day or two. Sincerely yours,

The shifting of all the records from Seattle to Curtis' New York address indicates his intent to make New York his headquarters. On the subsequent occasions that he visited Seattle he lived at the Rainier Club, listing it at his Seattle address from 1916 to 1920.

Schwinke's concern over the financial difficulties of the film company continued. He wrote Curtis again on 26 May: "Asahel [Curtis] asked me the other day about their bill for pictures made for the Head-Hunters while showing here, and says he is badly in need of the money. If I remember rightly, it is somewhere around $130.00. Mr. Albert has the bills, or at least I sent them to him. Can I make him any sort of a promise, or can a part of it be paid?"

On the previous day Schwinke had written to his friend and colleague, W. E. Myers, who was in the field in southern California collecting ethnographic data for *The North American Indian.*

Dear Myers: I sent you the Haida and Nootka manuscript Saturday, by registered mail. . . .

I don't know any news outside of what I have created myself. I am leaving the Chief at the end of the month. Some work he is now planning on doing is to take a year to finish. I had been thinking rather aimlessly about leaving, and when it came to the question of staying another year (to which I would be committed if I stayed at all) or leaving immediately, I decided. I don't know yet just what I will do, but I am going to loaf a few weeks, absolutely secure from telegrams and things. The reason I usually give for leaving is that Curtis has been paying me as much as I am worth to him, and that I am looking for a field where there is more room.

I hope the various delays have not inconvenienced you too much. The Studio has been taking the University pictures for their yearbook, and there seemed no other way but for me to help. They could not have afforded to hire another man. I have done an awful lot of work, and incidentally gained a lot of experience. Don't be surprised if I turn into a photographer. I will have my mail come to the Studio for a month or two, I suppose. Hope everything is fine with you. Sincerely yours,

On June 7 Schwinke was paid $525.00 for three months' salary and expenses in connection with *The North American Indian* and on 15 June 1915, he wrote an interesting letter to Myers that sheds additional light on the nature of his work and importance to Curtis.

Dear Myers: Your letter of the 8th came a few days ago. I had intended to send you the Kodak films you ask about, but I notice your letter does not say to do that, so in order that they will be perfectly safe I will place them in a legal envelope with your name on the outside, and leave them in the vault in the same compartment with the copy of the Nootka manuscript. You will undoubtedly be the first to look up that manuscript. I find twenty films, and as they were numbered consecutively, and no numbers are missing, they must be all there.

I notice you don't think much of photography as a vocation. You may rest assured, however, that [mine] will not be motion photography. I have had enough of that to last me at least three lifetimes. If you can suggest anything more logical than photography, though, I should be glad to hear of it. I believe I have the chance to get started right and develop a well paying business. Other men have made money at it, and I don't see why I can't. Also there doesn't seem to be any other line of business that interests me at all. What else would you do under those circumstances? The best I could do at present in any other line would be to start at the bottom, and there will still be plenty of time to do that if my contemplated venture should not prove a success. My first move will be to get into some place where I can get some practical experience at operating. Then for the big plunge.

This letter with other evidence we have accumulated indicates that Schwinke, not Curtis, took the Kodak pictures. Schwinke with his own 1903 Eastman Kodak (which is now in the Burke Museum) took photographs of Curtis with his informants and actors, Indian scenes, and Indian portraits. Moreover, Schwinke was the motion picture cameraman for *In the Land of the Head-Hunters*. Curtis established the camera position and directed the actors through his interpreter, George Hunt, but Schwinke operated the motor camera.

The letter also supports our notion of the team of which Edward Curtis was the Chief. Schwinke did the field work among the Makah, W. E. Myers wrote the report on Nootka and Haida incorporating Schwinke's material on the Makah, and Frederick Webb Hodge did the final editing. Curtis took the still photographs for the volume, gave final approval as Chief and did promotional work and fund raising.

Edmund Schwinke did not leave Seattle. After enjoying a summer of sailing, camping, backpacking, and canoeing, he became a partner in the "McBride Studio (E. E. McBride, Edmund Schwinke) Portrait Photographers." In 1917 Schwinke moved to Oak Hill, Ohio, where he subsequently married, served overseas in World War I, and returned to Oak Hill to become a successful businessman and pillar of the community. He lived a long and eventful life. We do not know if he ever got his money out of *In the Land of the Head-Hunters*. The last letter we have from Curtis to Edmund Schwinke, which does not sound promising, was written 8 June 1916.

Dear Schwinke: Pardon my apparent neglect in answering your letter. I have put it off hoping I would have something more definite to say. Matters have been particularly trying this winter, but just at the moment prospects look fairly good. I trust that, in the not too distant future, I will be able to take care of some of my obligations.

As to the Film Co: we have sued the World Film for $148,000 and anything else the court might see fit to give us but like all legal matters it will be rather long and drawn out. So far we have never had one cent on the picture and I am now endeavoring to carry through other activities which will give us our money back in the corporation. I assure you, I am doing everything in my power to work the matter out. It is going to take a bit of hustling on my part and a little patience from those who are interested.

Myers is just starting into the field and just how soon I will be able to get out is something of a question. I trust that everything with you will work out nicely.

With very kind regards, I am Sincerely Yours, Edward S. Curtis

These letters record the continuing financial difficulties of those whose early faith in the motion picture project had caused them to give their time and effort, as well as their money. Curtis seems to have been absorbed in trying to recoup his (and others') losses, and nothing is known to have come of his plan to make fifty-two movies of scenic places of North America. He did, however, continue with his schedule for *The North American Indian*.

Edward and Clara Curtis were divorced in 1919. From this time, when Curtis moved to California, there were two Curtis studios on the West Coast, one in Seattle and one in Los Angeles. Curtis and his daughter Beth ran the Los Angeles studio; and Clara Curtis and her sister, Sue Gates, operated the Seattle studio from 1919 to 1927. In 1928 Clara's daughter Katherine assisted in the operation, and finally in 1930 Joseph E. Gatchell purchased the studio from Clara Curtis.

Nineteen hundred and twenty-seven was a memorable year for Curtis. He made his last expedition, this time to Arctic Alaska, where he gathered material for the last volume in his series. His work there was reported in the Seattle *Post-Intelligencer* (1 September 1927):

Safe after six weeks of battling with Arctic storms, Edward S. Curtis, Seattle author and Indian authority, at the wheel of his fifty-foot craft, is today headed again into the hazards of Bering Sea, in a new and final quest.

Curtis' latest adventure came close to being his last. Caught by ice floes off Nunivak Island, where he was studying native life, the little vessel bearing Curtis, his daughter Beth, and J. S. Eastwood, was carried toward the Siberian coast and threatened destruction. For three days and nights Curtis remained at the wheel until danger passed.

On another occasion, faced by a water shortage, Curtis was forced to head into the teeth of a gale so fierce that it took him forty-eight hours to make the five miles into port.

But the expedition has been crowned with success, the adventurer said, for on Nunivak Island he discovered a tribe of natives conforming implicitly to old tribal laws and customs—the last group in the world, he believes, that is practically untouched by civilization.

The sequence of events in Seattle following this tour was relished by reporters writing in extravagant style of Curtis' arrest and incarceration half an hour after he walked ashore from the S. S. Almeda. From the Seattle *Post-Intelligencer* of 12 October 1927 comes this version:

In a fashion as unexpected to him as it was dramatic in its denouncement, Edward S. Curtis . . . made a startling, if humiliating reappearance in Seattle . . . after an absence of more than seven years. . . .

Vehemently protesting, he was taken to the county jail by deputy sheriffs and operatives of the Burns Detective Agency. After being locked up in a cell, he was shown an affidavit, signed by his divorced wife, Clara J. Curtis, proprietor of the Curtis photographic studio . . . in which she alleged he has been in contempt of court these past seven years for failure to pay alimony which has now accrued to the tune of $4,500.

After spending about two hours in jail Curtis came up with the two thousand dollars in bond for his release. An article in the Seattle *Post-Intelligencer* of 14 October 1927 indicates that Clara and Edward had been involved in eighteen to twenty court actions brought by one or the other during the past eight years. The press apparently lost interest in his court appearance when neither side was able to produce the original divorce decree, and the denouement of the case is not known. Curtis soon returned to California where he spent the rest of his long life.

By the end of 1930 all twenty volumes of *The North American Indian* had been published. These volumes and Curtis' photographs are an enduring monument to him. He died in 1952 in Los Angeles. He was eighty-four years old.

"My father was a man with great singleness of purpose," his daughter Florence has said.

When he was working on any phase of his photography career, he was never to be dissuaded from his main objective. At home in Seattle he was either searching for data, getting equipment and material ready for a field trip, or improving on his processes of photography and printing. And when we thought he might be coming home, he was in New York getting money or looking after the details of the book publishing. We always said he had no home life at all.

All this meant, of course, great sacrifice of the things most people need to lead a satisfying life—participating in sports, recreation, gardening and other avocations, but father didn't seem to need those safety valves. He was big, six feet two inches, husky, ruggedly built yet with this he had a soft voice with a pleasing tone to it that inspired confidence.

He was a driver, . . . yet never with money in mind except what he needed to carry on the work. At the time we didn't think of him as a genius but later, with proper perspective, we knew he was. Like most great men he seemed to have little sense of personal gain. Everything he did was directed toward the main theme of preparing material for The North American Indian and other writings about the tribes. His life was certainly dedicated to an ideal [Andrews 1962:53].

Appendix 1.   The Continental Film Company

Associated with several of Seattle's leading business men, Mr. Edward S. Curtis has formed a small company for the making of commercial motion pictures of the Indian and the Indian life.

Through his remarkable knowledge of this subject, Mr. Curtis will be able to make pictures which could be secured in no other way, and owing to his international standing as one associated with the Indian, the marketing of such pictures will be comparatively easy, and the demand a large one.

The profits to be had from such pictures are quite large, and exceptionally substantial dividends can be depended upon.

In forming a company for this purpose, Mr. Curtis feels that he is giving his friends an opportunity to participate in the advantage of the standing he has built up through many years of hard and careful work, and at the same time the capital furnished by such a corporation will make it possible for him to take advantage of the present world-wide demand for such pictures as he is so logically qualified to make.

During the last two years Mr. Curtis had made a careful study of the motion picture subject and the marketing of the product, in the course of which investigation he has fortunately had the confidence and received the advice of the foremost men in the field. Also he has consulted with many of the country's leading scientists and educators, and they are most enthusiastic in regard to the making of such a series of pictures. There is no question that every educational institution in the land will be interested in its success.

For the present the more important activities of the company will be the making of a complete series of motion pictures of Indians and Indian life. All this work is to be done by or under the immediate supervision of Mr. Curtis, who is so well known in association with his great pictorial work dealing with all tribes of Indians.

A series of pictures such as Mr. Curtis proposes to make will be of the greatest national importance—something of permanent educational and historical value. More than that, it should be exceptionally profitable. The production of motion pictures is a most profitable undertaking, and great as is the business today, it is but in its infancy. Genuine Indian pictures will be far more valuable than regular dramatic subjects. The reason for this is that the regular motion pictures have a life of but a few months, usually six. At the end of that time they go to the junk pile. The Indian pictures, owing to their historical and ethnological importance, will remain in existence for all time: rather than being junk in six months, they will become of increasing value, paying a dividend on the cost for years to come.

It is Mr. Curtis' purpose and desire to include in the series all the tribes of America, both North and South. These pictures, while made to meet the demands of the scientist and students, will at the same time be so rendered that they will possess the interest needed to make the tastes of the masses or those who are looking for amusement only. Mr. Curtis' experience as a lecturer fits him to grasp the wants of the amusement-seeking public.

In the making of this series of motion pictures of Indian life, there is a great work which Mr. Curtis can do as no other man can. He is backed by a lifetime of experience with this subject, and has the peculiar ability to handle the primitive people in a way which means success.

The questions might be raised as to whether the documentary material would not lack the thrilling interest of the fake picture. It is the opinion of Mr. Curtis that the real life of the Indian contains the parallel emotions to furnish all necessary plots and give the pictures all the heart interest needed. In this respect it is as important that we take into consideration the Indian's mental processes as it is to picture his unique costume.

To do the work in a way creditable to the subject and to the nation would require a vigorously conducted campaign covering a period of five to fifteen years, this presumably to include Central and South America. All pictures made should be classed among the educational, and should be preserved as a part of the documentary material of the country. It is needless to say that such a collection of material would be an important national asset, and would from the beginning have the encouragement of every educational institution.

In making such pictures, the greatest care must be exercised that the thought conveyed be true to the subject, that the ceremony be correctly rendered, and above all, that the costumes be correct. It must be admitted that the making of such a series of pictures would be the most difficult thing attempted in motion photography, but it can be done, and will be one of the most valuable documentary works which can be taken up at this time.

The Indians and the Indian life do now and will for all time furnish an important part of the literature, art, and drama of our country.

As to motion pictures and their bearing on the subject, it is safe to say that properly produced under proper and permanent arrangement, they can be made of more importance than books or printed illustrations.

The market for motion pictures is very large. This will be particularly so with those made by one with a world-wide reputation. Not only would there be a market in the United States and Canada, but in Europe and South America as well. The commercial advantage of the motion picture producing business is that the market is world-wide, with but a trifle taken from any one. It is, in fact, but a small tax upon the people of the world. Those who have not kept in touch with motion picture matters can have but a slight idea of the magnitude of the business. Many millions of people daily visit the motion picture theatres in the United States. There are more than 25,000 motion picture theatres in the country, and if these averaged but 2,000 admissions in a day it gives an almost unbelievable total. The fact of such a very large attendance means that the greatest single influence in our country today is the motion picture. Likewise, no other business reaches so great a number of people.

Mr. John Collier, of the National Board of Censorship of motion pictures, says: "A new kind of book has been produced and is being read by millions of people daily. The motion picture is a book, and an acted play, and a scenic wonderworld in one. It is more popular today than our public libraries, and it should concern the educational and religious agencies more than the printed book for the reason that motion pictures, being a form of drama, nearly always have a moral or immoral lesson to convey. Whether it be sermons, or educational lectures, or temptations to wrong-doing, each and all of these things can be conveyed more vividly through motion pictures than through printed books." (John Collier was Commissioner of Indian Affairs 1933–45.)

To sum it all up, the subject treated is one of the most interesting, the business is one of the most profitable of the day, the market world-wide, the man doing the work personally known to you and of international reputation.

The plans for the present are that all pictures made will be special feature subjects of from three to six reels in length. As to the marketing, there are two feasible methods. The first is to sell them by the state rights plan. By this method each subject should pay a profit of $25,000 to $50,000 within a year of its production, and two pictures a year should be produced. The second and best plan is to make pictures of six reels in length, make the strongest and most important production possible, and then booking the picture to be played in first class theatres throughout the United States. In fact, tentative arrangements have been made for so marketing the Indian pictures made by Mr. Curtis. This plan means putting on the road from ten to twenty sets of the film, and playing in each city a week or more with a return engagement ninety days later. Such booking of the pictures will be made through one corporation in New York, to cover the United States, and on a percentage basis. A moderately successful picture should pay a minimum profit the first year of $100,000, and one that proved particularly successful a profit of many times that. As an illustration, with a minimum of ten pictures playing at a profit of $100 a night from each picture, it is easy to see what the profit would be, and such an estimate is less than half what could rightly be expected.

Appendix 2.   In the Days of Vancouver

A documentary picture of the Kwakiutl tribes, the natives of Vancouver Island.

Captain Vancouver visited this region in 1792. The picture treats the natives as seen by him at that time.

SUB READER: (name of character and descriptive words)

Scene 1: Bust of first character.

(In this way treat some ten principal characters later to be seen in the picture. Examples: Tribal Chief; Pahala or Medicine-man; The Whale Medicine-man; The Chief's daughter. Scenes 1 to 10 inc.)

READER: "The Invocation."

Scene 11: Young man on high cliff or promontory, making a large prayer-fire. Fire and figure outlined against the sky, the aim being to have a magnificent picture as well as one dramatically striking. Man is fasting, and implores the divine ones for a vision and spiritual power. Different visions may appear in smoke. Faster has dropped asleep, and in the smoke is seen a vision of a young woman. He awakes and exits.

READER: "The vision is a reality."

Scene 12: Faster stands on a rocky shore. Sees canoe approaching on water in background. The occupant is the chief's daughter, who now becomes the heroine. When she comes closer she looks at him, and he sees that she is the girl he saw in the vision. She paddles on, and out of picture to the side. He steps to water, unties canoe fastened to rock, and follows in the direction she took.

Scene 13: Two canoes landing. Chief's daughter and faster step out of them and walk toward forest. Sub-chief, a man of about forty, who is a pahala or evil medicine-man, is concealed behind rocks, and watches the lovers as they land and walk away.

Scene 14: Lovers in forest sitting on log or rock. Pahala is seen watching them from concealment in shrubbery.

READER: "Medicine-men plot to destroy the faster, so the Pahala can have the Chief's Daughter."

Scene 15: Scene in forest. Three or four men plotting against the life of the faster, one exits.

Scene 16: Man who left the group in scene 15 is seen speaking with a woman, asking her to help them. (Will now term her villainess.)

Scene 17: (Back to 15) Medicine men still there. Enter the one who appears in 16. Shortly also the villainess. She is told what is wanted of her.

Scene 18: Hero again fasting. Villainess enters. Tells him of her love. He repulses her, insisting that he has no love for her, and that he is not now thinking of women and the world, but of spiritual things. In anger she exits.

Scene 19: Night scene. Faster has dropped to sleep. Villainess slips up, cuts off a lock of his hair, and takes trinkets from his neck. She exits.

READER: "On awaking he realizes that articles have been taken from him for the purpose of destroying his life by sorcery."

Scene 20: Wakes up and discovers that hair and trinkets have been taken. Hero is filled with fear, knowing the purpose is to kill him.

Scene 21: (Back to medicine camp in forest) Enter villainess with lock of hair and other articles. Men take toads, cut them open, and insert hair, etc., in bodies of toads. Place one in notch of tree, and another in ashes of fire.

READER: "The formal marriage proposal."

Scene 22: Two important men of tribe and clansmen of the hero, dress as wolves, and carrying ornamental staffs go to the home of the chief's daughter, and propose that she be given in marriage to the youth. In this scene the men enter a canoe and start on their journey to the neighboring village.

Scene 23: Their landing. They exit toward village.

Scene 24: They enter home.

Scene 25: Inside. Girl's family know of their coming, and are prepared. Scene shows interior of important house with great totem house-posts. Exchange of tokens or pledges.

READER: "The marriage is arranged, and the parties being important ones, a new home establishment is decided upon."

Scene 26: Man cutting giant tree in forest, with primitive wedges and chisels. Tree falls.

Scene 27: Men begin to work trunk of tree into shape for house timbers.

Scene 28: Making planks.

Scene 29: Transporting timbers.

Scene 30: Carving totem houseposts.

READER: "Material assembled, the house is built."

Scene 31: Setting house-posts.

Scene 32: Raising supporting timbers into place. (These timbers are about twenty inches in diameter and eighty to a hundred feet in length.)

Scene 33: Placing outer planks.

Scene 34: Placing roof planks.

READER: "Ceremonial dedication of house."

Scene 35: Dedication (This can be made short by including but a few of the many parts of the dedication rite, or it can be made long by including many of the important dances. We will presume it to cover five parts of the ceremony.)

READER: "The Wedding Party."

Scene 36: This is a pageant-like ceremony. The groom, with many canoe-loads of tribesmen, goes to the village of the bride. In this scene the party assembles at the shore, in gala costume, and embarks.

Scene 37: Fleet of canoes passing.

Scene 38: Landing at the bride's village.

Scene 39 to 48 (inc): Details of marriage ceremony depend on individual clan or personal medicine, but make a picturesque affair in any form. We will presume this to include five scenes and five dances. The dances at night will close the day.

READER: "Rival village prepares for war."

Scene 49: Warriors assembling on beach, displaying war implements.

Scene 50: The embarkment, which is in a measure ceremonial and according to fixed forms. Female relatives stand upon beach.

READER: "The attack upon the fishing party."

Scene 51: (As the party continues on its way they from time to time sight small parties and destroy or capture them. The object is to show the different activities as well as to give a true story of a war expedition.) In this scene we first see fishing party of men and women in small bay. Suddenly they see war canoes beating down upon them. They start to escape. War canoes follow and overtake fleeing fisher folk. Fight occurs in canoes. People in fishing canoes are killed or captured. The capsized canoes are seen floating on the water. (Killing is done in such a way that it cannot offend—handled as war, not as murder.) Captives are taken, hands and feet tied, and thrown into war canoes.

READER: "The devilfish catchers."

Scene 52: A party on a rocky shore, hunting devilfish. These fish live in burrows under large boulders, covered at high or medium tide and exposed at low water. The natives capture them by punching into the holes with small poles, until the angered creatures rush out. Picture should show enough of the octopus capture to get the attention of the audience. Then the approaching war party will be sighted. The octopus hunters, men and boys, flee to the forest. The war party lands, and follows. No killing is seen but heads are brought back and thrown into canoes. Two youths who were with fishermen are brought out as captives, to be kept as slaves.

READER: "The Clam Diggers."

Scene 53: Party on shore digging clams, mostly women. Some young and good looking. On sighting war party, all flee to forest. Pursued by warriors. (Flash.) Warriors merge from forest, with prisoners and perhaps a few heads. Prisoners are women, and are tied hand and foot. Are usually carried by throwing over the shoulders like sacks of flour. At times they are allowed to walk, but are hand tied, and led by ropes.

READER: "The attack upon the village."

Scene 54: (This is the village where the wedding occurred.) The war party has heard of the beautiful daughter of the chief, and each of the head men is secretly desirous of being the one to capture her. It is a night scene. The war party brings canoes close to the shore, and begins the attack. Implements are slings, bows and arrows, spears, and clubs. Also some of the men carry boxes containing fire, in order to set fire to the house. A vigorous attack is made upon the village.

Scene 55: Interior of house during pillage.

Scene 56: Chief's daughter is captured and carried away, to canoe.

Scene 57: A rival warrior steals the Chief's daughter and takes her to his canoe. A scrimmage between the two warriors, and the Captive is taken to the canoe of her original captor.

Scene 58: Village burning. This effect can be accomplished by burning one of the large houses.

READER: "Friends find the young man and save his life."

Scene 59: Opens with young man (seen in fasting pictures) wounded lying in underbrush. Friends, who have also escaped, find him, make him comfortable, and start building rude shelter.

READER: "The coming of Vancouver, at the village from which the war party started."

SUB-READER: "The Sing Gamble Game."

Scene 60: Group of eight or ten men are playing this game, which is a particularly vigorous one. Men are nude except for loin-cloth. Women and children come up and look on. Youth enters in great excitement, falling. Too excited to tell story. Finally makes it known that he has seen approaching a great monster. All exit toward promontory.

Scene 61: Party gathers on high bluff overlooking bay. They mill about, and at last form statuesque group, all gazing out to sea.

Scene 62: Vancouver's ship is seen in the distance, sails up, and nearing village. As they come fairly close sails are dropped, and ship anchors.

Scene 63: Explorers approach shore in small boat and land. Indians come down to them, but show much fear. Gifts are distributed. Indians invite the explorers to enter the village. All exit.

READER: "War party returns."

Scene 65: Great excitement in village. Indians accompanied by explorers run toward the shore.

Scene 66: Village party on shore, watching fleet of canoes as it enters bay. This gives us a picture showing the ceremony in connection with the return of a victorious war party.

Scene 67: War party walking toward village. Slaves are being led or dragged, heads carried, and the bodies of comrades who have been killed in battle are borne to the village.

Scene 68: Party enters great ceremonial house.

READER: "Dance of Victory."

Scene 69: Different individual dances are shown.

Scene 70: Captive girl (chief's daughter) is brought forward, and there is considerable discussion as to what is to be done with her. Many demand her life, owing to the injury which has in the past been inflicted upon them by her father. Her captor, the head chief, decides to have her dance, in order to determine whether she is really sufficiently attractive to be spared. She is a beautiful dancer, and this brings in one of the most effective of their dances. She proves so attractive that her life is to be spared.

READER: "Preparing their dead for burial."

Scene 71: Burial party. Large party of canoes going to the island of the dead.

Scene 72: Landing of burial party, and placing coffins in trees.

READER: "Vancouver spends day in sight-seeing."

Scene 73: Cooking in wooden utensils by use of hot stones.

Scene 74: Flattening heads of infants.

Scene 75: [illegible]

Scene 76: Placing totem pole, ceremonials.

Scene 77: Weaving blankets.

Scene 78: Curing fish.

Scene 79: Totem house front. Toward the end of the day explorers are shown entrance of one of their great ceremonial houses, the doorway of which is some strange, grotesque bird. This is a mechanical contrivance worked by men in concealment. As a person approaches it, the beak or mouth opens, and the man steps in. He is apparently swallowed. And so on, one person after another. On this night there is to be a great dance. It is the season when they naturally give their ceremonial dances, and they start it now, that the explorers may see the strange rites.

Scene 80: Messengers going about village announcing the ceremony.

Scene 81: The hamatsa or mummy-eating priest, in the forest preparing mummy.

Scene 82: The hamatsa dancing on his emergence from forest.

Scene 83: The hamatsa entering house with mummy.

Scene 84: Hamatsa dancing in house.

Scenes 85 to 94: Other dances are now given, many being striking trick performances, such as burning people alive. Give perhaps ten such.

Scene 95: At end of night ceremony Vancouver's men are seen to go to small boats and row toward ship.

READER: "Exploring party sails."

Scene 96: Morning scene, ship weighs anchor and departs. Many Indian canoes about, watching them.

Scene 97: While natives are watching explorers depart, chief's daughter slips from room, unties young slave, and tells him to go to their home with a message that she is alive and in the chief's house, and that she will each night try to leave the secret door unfastened, that her husband can come and steal her away.

Scene 98: Boy slips away.

Scene 99: Takes canoe and is gone.

Scene 100: He comes to home village, gives package and message to the husband, who has practically recovered. The husband urges his companions to go with him to retake his wife. They agree to do so. Small slave boy goes with them to show the way.

Scene 101: Party starts in canoes.

Scene 102: Landing at night. Husband and boy slip away, others stay with canoe.

Scene 103: Inside view of room where chief's daughter sleeps. Chief and the woman are shown, both apparently asleep. Woman cautiously raises [sic] up to make certain that the man is sleeping, then slips from couch, and unfastens small door. Again lies down. Soon she hears the door open. Young husband cautiously enters. They slip out together.

Scene 104: They enter canoe and start flight.

Scene 105: Sleeping room again. Chief wakes up, misses woman, sees open door, is very angry.

Scene 106: Wakes up other occupants of the house.

Scene 107: Ten or twelve men rush from house and go to canoe. On the moonlit water they have a glimpse of the fleeing canoe.

Scene 108: Pursuers quickly take canoes and start.

Scene 109: Fugitives realize that they are followed, and in desperation turn side to try to escape through whirlpool rapids.

Scene 110: Pursuers reach the promontory at turning point, and hesitate at attempting such rough water. Chief urges them to do so.

Scene 111: Fugitives are seen shooting through rapids.

Scene 112: Pursuing canoe is seen entering the bad water. They hit a rock, turn over, and are drowned.
(Finis)

Appendix 3. Outline for Scenario

(of a three to five-reel (3000 to 5000 ft.) Motion Picture, it being presumed that this can be arranged for a full evening's entertainment or for a shorter time if needed).

On the shores of the North Pacific is the title of the coming dissolving effect. The opening picture is of a woman paddling her canoe along the moonlit waters, half in the shadow of the somber forest which touches the water's edge in the way of this region. As her canoe glides silently through the waters she hears the revelry of the village which she is approaching. There appears the moonlit village with its long line of totem poles, and the fires gleaming before and in the many houses. Then we see approaching the village across the moonlit waters the visiting chief with the head-men of his tribe. They are singing songs of pride and greeting, and are answered by songs of welcome from the village.

The Story

Motana, son of Kenada (Watsulis), falls in love with Naida, daughter of Waket (Paas). The Sorcerer, brother of Yaklus (Yilis), also desires her, and plots to kill Motana. While Motana sleeps, the Sorcerer's niece steals his neckband and a lock of hair. He reports this evident attempt on his life to his father, who sends men to demand Naida and to kill the Sorcerer. Yilis village is attacked, and the head of the Sorcerer is brought to Waket.

Bethrothal of Motana and Naida; building of house for them; dedicatory feast and dancing. Bridegroom's party goes to Paas; sham battle; wedding; return to Watsulis.

Yaklus sends warparty to avenge his brother. Killing or enslavement of clam diggers, fisherman, devilfish hunters. Attack on Watsulis at dawn. Capture of Naida, death of Kenada, wounding of Motana. The warparty returns to Yilis and a dance of victory is held. (Various masked characters.) Naida sends a fellow captive to beg Motana to rescue her. He is pursued, but escapes and reaches home. Motana raises a small party, rescues Naida, is pursued by Yaklus, whose canoes are overwhelmed in rapids.

Shooting Schedule

30 men, 20 women, painted canoes

		[sequence of scenes]
o	*At Watsulis*	
n	Village street	16
e	Return of Motana	54
	Talk with Kenada	55
d	Departure of canoes	56
a	Canoes en route	57
y	Landing for night	58
	Messenger canoe leaves fleet	59
	" " rejoins fleet	62
	Fleet puts to sea	63
	Departure of bridegroom's party	33

o	Wedding canoe returns with bride	93
n	View of totem pole	94
e	Entering the Raven's mouth	95
d	*At Red Bluff*	
a	Thunderbird dancer in canoe	85
y	Close approach of canoes	87

o	*At Blunden Harbor* (take over 2	
n	new totems)	
e	Attack on Yilis	64–68
	Kenada brings back head	69
	Watchers on platform	84
	" " "	86

day	Canoe leaves shore	88	Medium-sized, painted canoe
	Sham fight on water	89	
	Bridegroom's party enters house	90	
one day	*At Kwaestums*		
	Hand-to-hand fight on a bluff	—	Camera in stern of pursuing canoe. Fugitives clamber up cliff. Two men plunge off into water.
	Scene revolving around tsonokwa	—	
	At Tsatsisnuqumi		
	Dances, 10–12 people, old house	—	
two days	*In artificial house of Waket*		
	Bethrothal gift	70	
	Women dances	71	
	Departure of bridegroom's party	72	Beach scene near house
	Paying for the bride	91	
	Carrying bride to canoe	92	
	In artificial house of Motana		
	Feast and dance in new house	82	
	In artificial house of Yaklus		
	Masked dances	121–126	
	Fire dancer	137	
	Display of heads and scalps	138	
	Demand the death of Naida	139	
	Naida dances before Yaklus	142	
	Thunderbird dismisses dancers	143	
	Yaklus discovers flight of Naida	160	
	Rush of people to the beach	161	
	Looting of a house	103	

30 men, 20 women, blackened canoes

one day	*At Watsulis*	
	Yaklus warriors swoop into bay	102
	Capture of Naida	104
	Naida dragged to canoe	105
	Fight between rival claimants	106
	Kenada killed	107
	Burning house, falling totem	108
	Victors depart	109
	Survivors find Motana, wounded	110
	Motana seeks Naida in flames	112
	Motana falls in the smoke	113
	Motana drags himself out	114
one day	*At Shell Island or Red Bluff*	
	Clam diggers	97
	The fishermen	98
	The devilfish hunters	99
	Warriors with gory head	100
	At some beach (supposedly Yilis) to be selected	
	Yaklus warparty assembling	96
	Returning war canoes	117
	War canoes, Naida and Slave	118
	Women dancing on shore	119
	Prisoners led to village	120

Appendix 4.   Filming the Head-Hunters

"Filming the Head-Hunters. How 'The Vanishing Race' Is Being Preserved in Moving Pictures." Strand Magazine, *American Edition, August 1915. Author anonymous.*

The greatest authority on the American Indian to-day is Edward S. Curtis, author of a monumental work entitled "The North American Indian," which, when completed, will consist of twenty huge volumes. This work is said to be the costliest book of the kind ever conceived, the net price per set being seven thousand five hundred dollars. Five hundred sets only will be published, and these will be distributed among the great libraries of the world and a few private "subscribers." When it is mentioned that for one single volume of this colossal work Mr. Curtis filled over one hundred quarto volumes of nearly a thousand pages each with his "notes" some faint idea will be obtained of the immensity of the task which the author has set himself to accomplish. Ten volumes only have been published up to the present, but Mr. Curtis confidently looks forward to the completion of the work during the next ten years. All the photographs used to illustrate this wonderful history of what Mr. Curtis is fond of calling "the vanishing race" have been made by the author himself, and they constitute some of the most remarkable pictures of tribal life ever made.

About four years ago Mr. Curtis began to employ the moving-picture camera to assist him in his work, and by its means he hopes to preserve for future generations the actual "life" of the North American Indian. He regarded the work from a purely educational standpoint, but in order to add to the interest he felt compelled to mix it with a little romance, which resulted in a very striking film entitled "In the Land of the Head-Hunters."

"All North American Indians," said Mr. Curtis to the writer, "have a strongly-developed sense of drama. Years ago I witnessed some of the performances with which the various villages entertain, each year, the people of other villages, and learned that a large part of the ability which results in the selection of a man as head-chief must lie in the direction of capacity for organizing these performances, as they have been organized and directed for centuries.

"I found that each ceremony selected for this strange dramatic representation belongs to the certain group which presents it, and that each part in each performance is taken by one who has a right to it through tribal law, or, possibly, through gift, and that each of the dramatic stories told in the great plays is based upon tradition or retells the tribal adventure, such as wars, notable love affairs, and so forth.

"I also found that while their plays are not written, they are prepared with almost as keen a sense of dramatic value as might be expected of the successful modern playwright, and that each spoken word, each bit of 'stage business' is passed from one season to another and from generation to generation with an amazing fidelity.

"I made the films of 'In the Land of the Head-Hunters' in British Columbia and Alaska, and they represent three actual years of work in the field by myself and my *aides*. We worked hard on that story, I can assure you. As you may well imagine, it was not an easy matter to link together in something resembling pageant form the many episodes which would best serve as revelations of true Indian character. Head-hunting, you must know, was formerly a constant practice among the Indians whose habitat ranged from Puget Sound to the Eskimo country. It is only within quite modern days that the terrifying custom has been abolished. However, head-hunting was but a detail of the lives of these extraordinary people. Greed and sacrifice, the love of man for woman, achievements in the hunt at sea or on land, were the real web and woof of their existence, coloured everywhere, as human psychology has ever been, by powerful religious influences.

"These people were sea-going, hardy, fearless, living on one of the most storm-bound coasts of the North Pacific. The resulting habits gave me an opportunity for such picturesque effects as no other primitive tribes could furnish, for the war-canoes of these Indians were as notable as the Roman galleys ever were. And a few of the originals remained to be used before my camera."

That there were many difficulties in making such a film it will be easily believed. Although Mr. Curtis had spent the better part of his life among the Indians and was looked upon almost as a "brother," he had to use much diplomacy and tact before he could overcome many of their scruples when it came to the recording of their national customs and ceremonies by means of the moving-picture camera.

"There were a thousand and one difficulties which I encountered in the production of the film," Mr. Curtis said, with a smile at the recollection. "It was utterly impossible, for instance, to get any Indian to wear a mask to which by birth and tribal custom he was not entitled. Other little difficulties, too numerous to mention—in themselves trivial, but requiring marvellous tact to handle—cropped up every day; but, after all, they only added to the interest of the work.

"What may be called the 'company' which 'produced' the drama under my direction was gathered in a curious way. I had become acquainted with George Hunt, a mixed-blood Kwakiutl, several years before, when I had studied and photographed the tribes for my books. This man gave me a great deal of help and assisted me in overcoming scruples which every 'actor' and 'actress' raised a dozen times a day. Before we settled upon any performer we had to establish the fact that that particular person was entitled to perform the part according to tribal rules and customs. Appearances did not decide upon the identity of our leading lady, although she was a very beautiful Indian girl; family history entitled her to play the part. And so, also, with the leading man and every other character down to the smallest.

"After I had pretty well formed my 'company' in the rough, and started their minds to work along the lines of the story I had fashioned with their help, I began to gather costume material and masks. This work carried me into remote places, and presently I found myself with a storehouse at Fort Rupert full of treasure trove. Such costumes as could not be obtained in the original were duplicated by Indian costume-makers out of Indian material. The animal masks used in the land ceremonies, and especially in the great war-canoe pageant, represent imaginary as well as living animals, and are the 'real thing,' being definitely sacred to the Indian; the great raven's head which swallows those who pass into the temple is an actual Indian device, built perhaps a century ago.

"It took months to break down the natives' prejudice against acting for such a purpose the ceremonies which they held as sacred, and the gathering of the company for its actual work meant my personal visits to each of the villages from which an actor or actress came, with, perhaps, long discussions and bargainings with the head men. Among the old medicine-men and chiefs also there was much opposition at our plan, for they felt that it entailed exposure of secrets they held sacred. Where scruples of this kind existed I found that money alone never overcame them.

"The search for our leading lady was unique. It was necessary that she should be high-caste, else she would not be permitted to enact the *role*, and when she was secured we found that high-caste has a meaning in Alaska as definite as that which it has in India. The girl could not even eat in the presence of the Indians of lower caste, and finally it was found necessary to serve her apart, in solemn state, with specially-prepared food. One branch of her family disapproved of her work with us entirely, and one morning, just as we were ready for work, it was found that they had kidnapped her, having stolen upon the village in canoes before dawn and borne her off against her will. Disaster threatened our play in consequence, but, not to be thwarted in our plans, we boarded a gasolene boat, overhauled the abductors, and recaptured our 'star.' This was an exciting episode, and I am sorry I was not able to film it, for the rescue was quite dramatic, as the abductors were loath to allow the lady to rejoin the company. However, everything was finally settled to mutual satisfaction, and no further attempts were made to deprive us of our leading lady. Our hero, though less difficult to 'manage' than our heroine, was by no means an easy problem. He had as much 'temperament' as any London or New York *matinee* idol, and we had all our work cut out to keep him good-tempered and open to reason. Finally we let him have pretty much his own way, and, as he was a born actor, the result was highly satisfactory. He was under twenty, and as finely formed and as strong as a human being could well be. I am sure he would create a sensation were I to bring him to New York!"

It is highly probable that "In the Land of the Head-Hunters" will prove the fore runner of other film stories dealing with tribal races. Mr. Curtis proposes doing one each year for the next ten years, going to different parts of the world for the purpose, and showing tribal life and drama among the so-called "savage" races of Africa, New Zealand, Borneo, India, etc. "In the Land of the Head-Hunters" is said to be the most carefully-worked out and accurate human document ever produced by means of the motion-picture camera. The scenes were taken in exactly the places where they are supposed to have been enacted. The war-canoes are actual war-canoes, while the village destroyed by fire is a real Indian town built by Indians. The totem-poles are actual totem-poles, Indian carved.

In speaking of this photo-drama Mr. Curtis gave the writer some very interesting information regarding the Kwakiutl Indians. "They practise," he said, "a most successful system of communal life, a system which has stood the test of time. All live for each other, and while one is wealthy no other one wants. They hold frequent *potlach* or 'giving-away' feasts—a ceremony which is unique among the Indians of the North Pacific Coast. Property given away at a *potlach* cannot be collected on demand, and need not be repaid at all if the one who receives it does not for any reason wish to requite the gift.

"When the recipient holds a distribution of property, however, he may return an equal amount, or a slightly larger amount, or a smaller amount, with perhaps the promise to give more at a later date. If a man at a *potlach* feast should insist on being paid what he had at some previous time given to the distributor, to say nothing of demanding interest, he would thenceforward be without influence in the tribe.

"The *potlach* is the basis of the whole Kwakiutl social system. It provides for a communistic life. No individual can starve or want so long as there is any property in the possession of the tribe, for there are always distributions of property, and if the individual is in need between the times of such distributions, he can always borrow at interest. When the principal and interest become due he simply, if still at odds with fortune, borrows another amount sufficient to pay. Thus he may continue piling up debts until payment is hopeless.

"The *potlach* is intimately bound up with the life of the family. Distributions of property are made whenever a name is changed, whenever a marriage is contracted, whenever a man accumulates a considerable amount of property and wishes to secure honour for his name and race.

"The explanation of the fact that with the enormous amount of 'business' done at the rate of one hundred to three hundred per cent the tribe has never found itself bankrupt is that no man can demand payment of debt without first showing good cause for the demand, and such cause can be found only in the expressed determination to perform some kind of public ceremony at which property will be given away. Thus any property paid as principal and interest will soon find its way back among the people; in fact, the debt is paid only on the day of the distribution, so that practically no time elapses with the bulk of the tribal property in the hands of one man.

"The feeling at the bottom of the *potlach* is that of pride rather than greed. Occasionally men are found who try to accumulate wealth by means of the *potlach* and by lending at interest, but the system has always swallowed them, simply because a man can never draw out all his credits and keep the property thus accumulated. He must first call all the people together and inaugurate a *potlach* before his debtors will pay him.

"Although he never profits by it in the end, a Kwakiutl Indian who has property is continually lending it out at interest. There are two kinds of native currency—a 'blanket,' which has the value of fifty cents in American money, and a 'copper,' which may be worth as much as sixty thousand dollars. The blankets, which are of the trade variety, and which were introduced long years ago by the Hudson Bay Company, have intrinsic value, of course, though they are seldom used for covering. But 'coppers' are currency backed by the wealth of the tribe. However, if a chief were to risk losing his reputation for liberality by trying to realize on a sixty-thousand dollar 'copper' he would find that the real property of the entire tribe would not come to this amount—that is, exclusive of real estate.

"Individuals have scant right, by tribal law, in real estate. It belongs not only to the living members of the tribe, but to future generations. For example, a trader whom I knew once sought to buy from a tribe a tract of land. The chiefs scorned his offer of heaps of silver dollars by replying: 'We do not rob the children unborn.'

"Whenever a 'copper' changes hands by sale, it doubles in value. 'Coppers' all have distinctive names. For example, the ancient chief who is Kenada [in] 'In the Land of the Head-Hunters' traces the history of a 'copper' called 'Tlaholamus,' or steel-headed salmon. This was brought to Fort Rupert in 1864 by a Haida chief and is greatly prized. The metal of a 'copper' is placer-mined, like placer gold—that is, 'panned out' from gravel in streams. The 'Tlaholamus' copper, brand new, sold for seventy blankets. Now it is worth six thousand blankets, having changed hands at various ceremonies. As recently as 1909 the equivalent of twenty thousand blankets was paid for a 'copper' called 'Mamuwila' meaning 'taking property out.' The price was paid in blankets, sloops, and cheaper 'coppers,' part real, part represented by the transfer of debts.

"Whenever a chief sells a 'copper' he has to distribute among the tribes the amount it realizes or for ever be disgraced. Financial advantage for the individual is altogether lacking. What he does earn is much 'highness' and a name like Nuh-na-lits-um-kilaq—'Born to be prodigal of his property.'

"A man without property can often pay his debts by the system known as *tsowelsu*, whereby he draws on the future. Knowing that he will receive a certain share at the next *potlach*, he transfers his rights to this share to his creditor. This is very much like the notes given to American moneylenders by American heirs whose inheritance is in trust. If an outsider—a half-breed, for example—lends money, he must be very careful to collect in negotiable security, when the debtor has it. Otherwise the debtor may say: 'I will pay my debt with *tsowelsu.*' And *tsowelsu,* when the next *potlach* comes, may be the transfer of a credit, not the receiving of actual property.

"Breaking a 'copper,' and thus impairing its value, is a ceremony of great moment. He who rivets together the pieces of a broken 'copper' and sells it loses prestige for himself and his tribe. But the purchaser gains honour, for the remade 'copper' is worth more than ever before. Sometimes 'coppers' are cast into the deep water. This brings great 'highness,' but really involves little loss of actual property to the individual, for 'coppers' may represent marriage debts, which, repaid in kind, would have to be distributed among the members of the tribe. You must understand that the matter of 'coppers' is strictly tribal business, and the credit they represent is practically what the Government puts behind as its paper currency. The whole effect of the *potlach* and 'copper' system is to make many individual Indians lazy and prodigal, and some are veritable parasites on the other members of the tribe.

"The Indians of the North Pacific shores are master-workers in wood. The great eighty-man war-canoes of "In the Land of the Head-Hunters" are all of primitive native work, and were made from huge cedars, hollowed out with fire and stone mauls and wedges. The largest cedars in the forest were picked out and cut down by making two cuts about thirty inches apart, the workman using a stone maul fitting the hand and a chisel consisting of a hard piece of yew protected at the head by a wrapping of cedar-bough rope, and with a sharpened stone, sometimes an iron, bound at the other end.

"Kwakiutl tribesmen are able to fell a tree more quickly with these primitive implements than white men with the keenest steel axes. As soon as the tree has fallen fire is laid to hasten the hollowing-out process. Then the natives, equipped with knives made of mussel-shell about ten to twelve inches long and four inches wide, with yellow cedar-bark along the hinge-edge, start shaping the prow and stern of the canoe, while others, with bone knives made by splitting out and sharpening a wide sliver from the leg-bone of a bear, work at digging out the interior of the craft. Sometimes women assist in the work, using a sharp bit of stone inserted in the end of a piece of yew, or an adze consisting of the blunt end of a strip of bone lashed to a handle of maple or apple wood. Wood workers also use a tapering bone-point gimlet mounted on the end of a wooden spindle, which is twirled between the palms.

"The making of a canoe requires many months. When it has assumed something of the shape intended, the half-finished canoe is brought to the beach and supported on blocks about two feet from the ground. When finally it has been moulded and polished the bottom is charred and then rubbed off with an old mat and scraped with a mussel-shell. Later it is thoroughly greased with goat or deer tallow.

"In fashioning their canoes and totem-houses," Mr. Curtis explained, "the Kwakiutl draw up no plans or specifications. Their natural sense of proportion and fitness of things is their only guide in the designing of their sometimes really beautiful homes. Their totem images are frequently of splendid imaginative quality and display a surprising fertility of invention. The canoes, houses, and carvings they make achieve symmetry and balance without any artificial aid to the workman's eye."

Two or three canoes with full complement of men were used in the catching of a whale, as shown in the photo drama. The whale is highly venerated. The Kwakiutl would not harpoon a "killer-whale" at all, for that is very bad "medicine." It is a "finback" that Motana brings back to shore in the picture. "And a mighty tough job it was," Mr. Curtis said, "for the whale put up a hard fight. Killing a ninety-foot amphibian and towing him back to shore is no easy morning's diversion, I can assure you.

"Before setting out to capture a whale," continued Mr. Curtis, "the young chief religiously bathes and scrubs in salt water and prays to the whale as follows: 'Great Whale, I know thine eye is upon me.' Sea-lions, which blacken the rocks eighteen and twenty miles out to sea, are not so highly venerated. They are harpooned from small canoes, which steal silently upon them.

"The fact that the young chief bathes so carefully before setting out to capture a whale brings up the matter of general ceremonial bathing. The boy destined to become a great chief is never permitted to touch warm water. Every day he is sent into the salt water, even if ice has to be broken. After his swim his father thrashes him soundly with a huckleberry besom!

"Fishing," concluded Mr. Curtis, "is the chief means of sustenance of these Indians. Of the various kinds of sea-food the devilfish is considered the greatest novelty and delicacy. Fresh caught, promptly killed, and properly cooked by a Kwakiutl woman, devilfish is mighty good eating, as I have proved on many occasions myself."

The story which Mr. Curtis has conceived in the film, "In the Land of the Head-Hunters," concerns a stalwart young Indian named Motana who sees in a vision a beautiful girl of high caste and promptly falls in love with the apparition. In order to prepare himself for the time when he shall see her in the flesh he kills a sea-lion and a whale and sleeps in a room containing a fine selection of skulls—to show his courage. Then Motana finds the maid of his dream and marries her, after which there is a tremendous battle, in which many heads are captured—or supposedly captured. Naida, Motana's bride, is captured by one of the enemy—Yaklus by name—who takes her to his village. They are followed by Motana, who recaptures his bride and flees with her in his canoe. Yaklus follows hot after them, and is led by Motana into a dangerous gorge, where his canoe is shattered and Yaklus drowned. Thus everything ends happily. The story, of course, is a minor detail, the real object of the film being to show the customs, amusements, fights, domestic life, and sports of the North American Indians. That it succeeds in doing this is proved by the rapt attention with which audiences follow the various exciting incidents that appear on the screen.

Appendix 5. The Old and the New

There are a number of differences between *In the Land of the Head-Hunters* as it was when acquired by the Field Museum and the 1973 restored version entitled *In the Land of the War Canoes*. Many of these differences have been described in the first four chapters. But in order to set the record straight and to keep historians in the art of the cinema from being misled, we wish to record other changes made by us in preparing the 1914 version of the Curtis film for the addition of the 1973 mixed sound track.

The 1973 version of the film has a large number of acknowledgments lacking in the old film. Whereas the original film opened with a title, "The Vigil of Motana," the new film opens on a scene of fast-moving canoes, one of which has a Thunderbird dancer in the bow. This scene is followed by still shots of Naida, Motana, Kenada, Waket, the Sorcerer, and Yaklus taken from Curtis' book, *In the Land of the Head-Hunters*. The old film at this point has only a still shot of Naida, which is followed by a view of sea lions on the rocks.

The next scene in both the new and the old versions shows Naida arriving by canoe, but in the new film some frames were omitted to soften the break between distant and near canoe images. The hunt for sea lions in the old movie end with Motana crouching on the rocks with his harpoon. In the new edition the scene ends with sea lions on the rocks.

The whale hunting episode in the old version ended with a scene showing Motana emerging from the mouth of the beached whale carcass. In the new movie this scene was removed.

Both the old and the new show Motana at his vigil, but in the new film the sleep scene has been darkened. In the scenes with the sorcerers, portions of the film considered by us to be too dark in the old film have been lightened in the new. Some scenes of Motana's return to his village have been lengthened in the new version by printing frames in sequence, then in reverse sequence.

The opening scenes of the wedding party have been altered somewhat. In the old film three canoes are seen approaching in the distance followed by the same canoes now moving very fast with the Thunderbird dancer in the lead canoe. This sequence has been reversed in the new edition.

The old footage of the fight on top of the cliff ended with the two participants struggling at the edge of the precipice. Indian informants remembered that the sequence ended with a dummy being thrown from the cliff and recommended that the scene be added. We did so in the new version and this is the only place in which there is any footage not actually directed by Edward Curtis.

The scene of the death of Kenada in the old film seemed overly long and even possibly comical by current standards. Accordingly it was shortened in the new.

In the sequence where Motana is rescuing Naida from the horrible Yaklus there were some changes of significance. Curtis filmed Motana opening the door, looking in and then entering and disappearing into the house. He then shot the same scene from inside the house showing Motana opening the door, entering the house, and arriving inside. We cut the film to show Motana part way into the house from the outside, and the rest of the way in the house from the inside.

The canoe chase at the end of the film was interrupted by a long sequence of surf and waves breaking on shore in the original film. This interruption was eliminated in the new version.

A major change between the old and the new was the elimination of the original Curtis titles of the silent movie and the addition of our new titles and sound track.

Appendix 6.   George Hunt's Account Book

masks Bought for Mr. E. S Curtes 191

Feb 17	1	Renxomt	thunder Bird	mask	4	00
"	"	1	BEgwesent	man of the sea	Do	8	00
"	"	1	Xosewe	wolf Dancer women	Do	1	50
Mar. 20	1	gweRemt	true whale	Do	15	00
"	"	1	RweRomt	Eagle Dancer	Do	4	00
"	"	1 g'omoRomt	monster cheep of the sea	Do	10	00
"	"	1	BeK!wesemt	wild man of the woods	Do	4	00
"	"	1	EdemRomt	cran	Do	10	00
"	"	1	g'omeselagemt	chief of the ghosts	Do	7	00
"	31	1	Hagaleka wegemt	cheep Docter	Do	4	00
april 29	1	gwaxomt	temsewato. Raven and sqirel	Do	7	50
"	"	1	Dsonag'wa	wild women of the woods	Do	4	00
"	"	3	yelxP.ayo	Double Headed snake	Horns	15	00
may 3	3	"	"	Do	15	00
"	"	1	noKemgelaga	winter Dance spirite Emege	8	00

$$ 117 \quad 00 $$
less.. $$ 15 \quad 00 $$
$$ 102 \quad 00 $$

gwelela naxnememoxE's

1	maE'mtagila	walker ahead People. sea gull
3	gexsEm	all Dressed cheefs
4	RweRwaK!wum	true smoke maker tribe
5	senL!Em	Beams of the sun tribe
6	laE'loxsE'ndayo	Breaker up of other tribe. war
7	ElgwEmwe	Blood on one side of them.
2	Toyalatawa	Peace Keepers tribe

masks Bought for Mr. E. S Curtes 1913

mar 7	#	1	HoxhoKwewe	Hamatso cranioxth mask		7	50
"	"	1	Hoxhogwedseve	"	Heaven Do	7	50
"	"	1 gelokwewe	"	Barbakwalonoxse Do	7	50
"	"	1 gEloqwedseve	"	Do Heaven Do	7	50
"	"	1	Do	"	Do	7	50
"	"	1	gxaxwewe	"	Raven Earth Do	7	00
"	"	1	gwodseye	"	Do Heaven Do	7	50
"	"	1	maxemt	Keller	whale Do	11	00
"	"	1	gweRemt	true	" Do	15	00
"	"	1	K!somagemt	Bull Head fish	Do	18	50
June 16	1	totem			90	50
"	"	1	totem	Oole	75	00
	1	RwaKwaKom	g'omoyewe	House	165	00

646	gweimailas Brother of	642 his wife 647	Lelelawek	noxEmatEgah
649	watewed	hes sisto 648	L'axL'aledzemga	
		" wife 650	Lelemox	Kietsona
		" Doughter 651	L'aletilakw	
		" son 652	melede	
	19 RwaKwaKom	gegelgem	House	
653	HawelRwalat	his wife 654	adaga	walebaye
655	wabedo son of 653	" " 656	waltasLala	Dyeng'ayo
		" son 657	Haxwoseme	
		" Doughter 658	yugo'Lasche	
659	Haxwaseme Brother of 653	his wife 660	maxwalaogwa	mamaleleg'em
		his sisto 661	max'mEwedzemga	
662	LelaKenes	" wife 663	L'emelxelageles	wewomasgem
		" Doughter 664	lexlegidzemga	
		" " 665	Rwenxwalaogwa	
666	Dadox Rweme Brother of 662	" wife 667	K'amaxalas	madetbe
668	L'agwadze son of 666	" wife 669	ciomak	nenelkenox
		" " 670	gweP'emgelokw	senL!Em
671	Ts.Ex'ede	" " 672	gwagwadaxeto	lalaxsendayo
		" Doughter 673	melede	
		" " 674	mentedaas	
		" " 675	gema	

Sample pages from George Hunt's account book, recorded in 1913–14 during the filming of *In the Land of the Head-Hunters*.

Bibliography

Andrews, Ralph W.
  1962   *Curtis' Western Indians*. Seattle: Superior Publishing Company.
Anonymous
  1911   Curtis interview. *New York Times*, 16 April.
  1915   "Filming the Head-Hunters. How 'The Vanishing Race' Is Being Preserved in Moving Pictures," *Strand Magazine*, American edition, August, pp. 106–16.
Barbeau, Marius
  1950   *Totem Poles*. Bulletin 119, vol. 2, National Museum of Canada, Ottawa.
Boas, Franz
  1897   *Social Organization and Secret Societies of the Kwakiutl Indians*. Report of the U.S. National Museum for 1895, Washington, D.C.
  1910   *Kwakiutl Tales*. Columbia University Contributions to Anthropology, vol. 2. New York: Columbia University Press.
  1921   *Ethnology of the Kwakiutl*. 35th Annual Report of the Bureau of American Ethnology, Washington, D.C.
  1930   *Religion of the Kwakiutl Indians*. Columbia University Contributions to Anthropology, vol. 10. New York: Columbia University Press.
Burroughs, John, John Muir, and George Bird Grinnell
  1901   *Alaska: Narrative, Glaciers, Natives*. Harriman Alaska Expedition, vol. 1. New York: Doubleday, Page and Company.
Bush, W. Stephen
  1914   " 'In the Land of the Head Hunters': Remarkable Motion Picture Produced by Edward S. Curtis, Famous Authority on North American Indians," *Moving Picture World* (New York) 22:1685.
Coleman, A. D., and T. C. McLuhan
  1972   "Curtis: His Work." Introduction to *Portraits from North American Indian Life* by Edward S. Curtis, pp. v–vii. New York: Dutton.

Curtis, Edward S.
  1906a   "Vanishing Indian Types: The Tribes of the Southwest," *Scribner's Magazine* 39 (May):513–29.
  1906b   "Vanishing Indian Types: The Tribes of the Northwest Plains," *Scribner's Magazine* 39 (June):657–71.
  1907–30 *The North American Indian*. 20 volumes. Vols. 1–5, Cambridge, Massachusetts; vols. 6–20, Norwood, Connecticut.
  1907   Vol. 1 —Apache, Jicarilla Apache, Navajo
  1908   Vol. 2 —Pima, Papago, Qahatika, Mohave, Yuma, Maricopa, Havasupai, Apache-Mohave
  1908   Vol. 3 —Teton Sioux, Yanktonai, Assiniboin
  1909   Vol. 4 —Apsaroke, Hidatsa
  1911   Vol. 5 —Mandan, Arikara, Atsina
  1911   Vol. 6 —Piegan, Cheyenne, Arapaho
  1911   Vol. 7 —Yakima, Klickitat, Interior Salish, Kutenai
  1911   Vol. 8 —Nez Perce, Walla Walla, Umatilla, Cayuse, Chinookan Tribes
  1913   Vol. 9 —Salishan Tribes of the Coast, Chimakum Quilliute, Willipa
  1915   Vol. 10—Kwakiutl
  1916   Vol. 11—Nootka, Haida
  1922   Vol. 12—Hopi
  1924   Vol. 13—Hupa, Yurok, Karok, Wiyot, Tolowa, Tutuni, Shasta, Achomawi, Klamath
  1924   Vol. 14—Kato, Wailaki, Yuki, Pomo, Wintun, Maidu, Miwok, Yokuts
  1926   Vol. 15—Southern California Shoshoneans, Dieguenos, Plateau Shoshoneans, Washo
  1926   Vol. 16—Tiwa, Keres
  1926   Vol. 17—Tewa, Zuni

1928   Vol. 18—Chipewyan, Cree, Sarsi

1930   Vol. 19—Wichita, Southern Cheyenne, Oto, Commanche

1930   Vol. 20—Nunivak, King Island, Little Diomede Island, Cape Prince of Wales, Kotzebue

1909   "Indians of the Stone Houses," *Scribner's Magazine* 54 (February):161–75.

1914   *Indian Days of the Long Ago.* Yonkers-on-Hudson, New York: World Book Company.

1915a   *In the Land of the Head-Hunters.* Yonkers-on-Hudson, New York: World Book Company.

1915b   *The Kwakiutl.* Portfolio and vol. 10 of *The North American Indian.* Reprinted 1970. New York and London: Johnson Reprint Company.

Dall, William H.; C. Keeler; H. Garrett; W. H. Brewer; C. H. Merriam; G. B. Grinnell; and M. L. Washburn

1901   *Alaska: History, Geography, Resources.* Harriman Alaska Expedition, vol. 2. New York: Doubleday, Page and Company.

Ewing, Douglas C.

1972   "The North American Indian in Forty Volumes," *Art in America,* July–August, pp. 84–88.

Flaherty, Robert J., and Frances Hubbard Flaherty

1924   *My Eskimo Friends "Nanook of the North."* New York: Doubleday, Page and Company.

Graybill, Florence Curtis, and Victor Boesen

1976   *Edward Sheriff Curtis: Visions of a Vanishing Race.* New York: Crowell.

Grinnell, George Bird

1905   "Portraits of Indian Types," *Scribner's Magazine* 37 (March): 259–73.

Halliday, William M.

1935   *Potlatch and Totem, and the Recollections of an Indian Agent.* London and Toronto: J. M. Dent.

Lindsay, Vachel

1922   *The Art of the Moving Picture.* New York: Macmillan Company. (Originally published 1915)

Marshall, Edward

1912   "The Vanishing Red Man" (interview of Edward S. Curtis), *Hampton Magazine* 28 (May):245–53, 308.

Meany, Edmond S.

1908   "Hunting Indians with a Camera," *World's Work* 15 (March):10004–11.

Mochon, Marion

1966   *Masks of the Northwest Coast.* Publications in Primitive Art 2, Milwaukee Public Museum.

Muhr, Adolph F.

1907   "E. S. Curtis and His Work," *Photo-Era,* July, pp. 9–13.

Oregon, Washington and Idaho Gazeteer and Business Directory, 1892

Rice, Leland

1976   *Edward S. Curtis: The Kwakiutl, 1910–1914.* University of California, Irvine.

Seattle City Directories, 1890–1932

Wilson, Edward Livingston

1881   *Wilson's Photographics: A Series of Lessons Accompanied by Notes, on All the Processes Which are Needful in the Art of Photography.* Philadelphia.

Who's Who is America, 1912–30

Index

Page numbers in *italic* refer to illustrations.

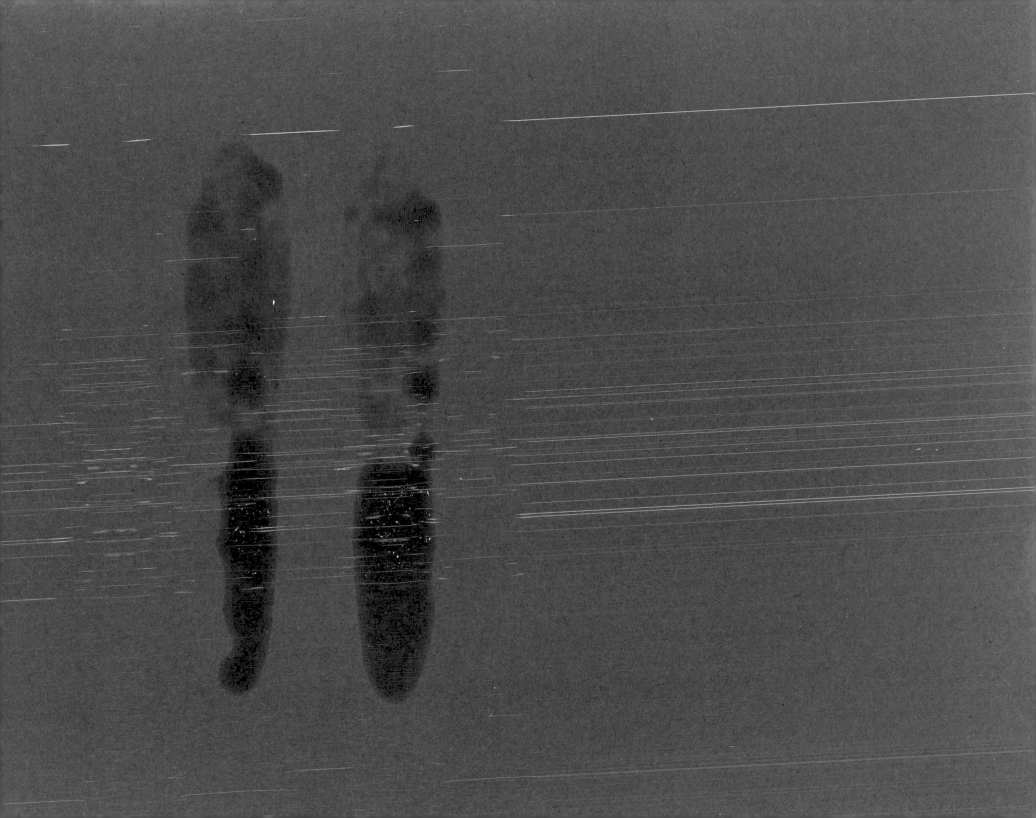